FODOR'S

FUN IN.

NEW ORLEANS

Honey Naylor

Published by
FODOR'S TRAVEL GUIDES
New York & London

ISBN 0–679–01356–3

Maps and plans by
Jon Bauch Designs, Mark Stein Studios, Pictograph
Illustrations by Diana Huff

New titles in the series

Maui
Rio

also available

Acapulco
Bahamas
Las Vegas
London
Montreal
New York City
Orlando Area
Paris
Puerto Rico
San Francisco
St. Martin/Sint Maarten
Waikiki

Contents

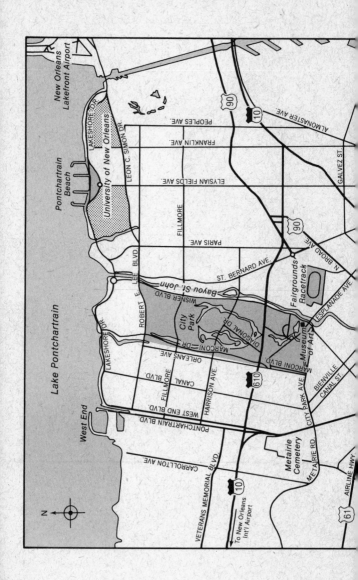

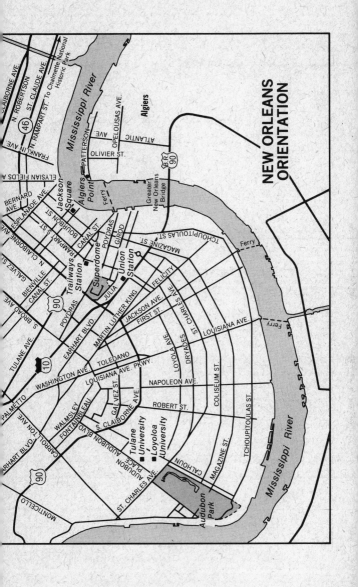

NEW ORLEANS ORIENTATION

Overview

Long ago, 110 miles inland from where it rushes out to meet the Gulf of Mexico, the Mississippi River carved out a piece of land in the form of a croissant. New Orleans, much of which is five feet below sea level, rides on this very flat crescent-shaped raft between the river and Lake Pontchartrain, thus one of its nicknames, the "Crescent City." (The city's other nickname is the "Big Easy," the origins of which should be obvious.) The four parishes (other states call them counties) of the greater metropolitan area sprawl over some 360 square miles, roughly 200 of which are more or less dry land. Of the 1,200,000 people in those four parishes, about half live in New Orleans proper.

New Orleans is the nostalgia capital of America. With its ambience, architecture, and Latin emphasis on things sensuous, it has much more in common with Rome, Marseilles, or Rio, than any American city. It is a very romantic city, very much in love with its exotic legends. Tales of pirates, voodoo queens, and the birth of jazz are as carefully preserved as the physical aspects of its 270-year history. Its party-town reputation is also nurtured and it is as well-founded as it is well-known.

No North American city comes close to New Orleans when it comes to celebrations. Six million annual visitors is just New Orleans's version of having a few friends in. In between Mardi Gras and other major annual bashes there are mini-festivals; in addition, brass bands frequently pop up out of nowhere and parade around town for no reason except that parading around town is a fun thing to do.

Riverboats play upon the Mississippi River, their great red paddles kicking up froth alongside serious tankers and other foreign vessels calling at America's largest port—the world's second largest, in terms of volume. The paradox is that New Orleans is both a major world city with a thriving port, and an old-fashioned small town with an insouciant, fun-loving soul that bedevils progressives bent on jerking it into the 20th century.

Orientation

There being no hills in these marshlands, the best place to orient yourself to the city is atop the very 20th-century International Trade Mart, at Canal Street and the river. For $2 ($1 for kids 6–12, under 6 free) you ride in a glass-enclosed elevator up the side of the building to Viewpoint, the observation deck on the 31st floor. On the deck there are huge photographs identifying the sights and placed so you can compare your view with the pictures, coin-operated telescopes, and a 360-degree panorama of one of the world's truly great cities.

Unless you want to drive yourself nuts you'd do well to forget—at least for now—about "north, south, east, and west." Because of the serpentine meanderings of the river, New Orleanians—known locally as locals—refer instead to riverside, lakeside, downriver (also called downtown), and upriver (uptown).

Standing with your back to the river and looking straight down you'll see on your right a broad, tree-lined boulevard running away from the water. That's Canal Street, the dividing line between uptown and downtown. To your right is downtown, and uptown rolls around to your left. Downtown, at the great bend of the river, the steeples of St. Louis Cathedral rise up over the sloping gray roofs of the French Quarter. Adjacent to the Quarter, the streets of Faubourg Marigny angle sharply to follow the river. (A *faubourg* is a suburb; the little Creole cottages in Marigny are located in one of the first areas to grow up outside of the Quarter.) Residential and industrial Bywater and Arabi hug the river beyond, and much further downriver are the green fields of Chalmette, where Andrew Jackson whipped the British in the Battle of New Orleans. Directly in front of you and fanning over to your left is the Central Business District—the CBD. You're standing on its foot. The vast blue of Lake Pontchartrain washes across the horizon. A 24-mile-long causeway stretches over it, linking the city with the piney woods and charming towns of St. Tammany Parish to the north. The great expanse of green beyond Canal Street to your right, near the lake, is City Park, covering 1,500 lush acres of the city's mid-section, Mid-City. Acres and acres of former sugar plantations spread out to your left, comprising the uptown sections of town and, far in the distance, Jefferson Parish. A couple of hundred miles beyond that is Lafayette, capital of bayou and Cajun country in southwestern Louisiana.

On the riverside side of Viewpoint, upriver, is the Greater New Orleans Bridge, linking the city's East Bank, where you are, to the West Bank, which is almost exactly due east of where you are. To your left, at the great bend, is Algiers Point, nemesis of riverboat pilots and ship captains. Between the bridge and the point (acrossriver, as it were) is Algiers, a very old, predominantly residential section of the city.

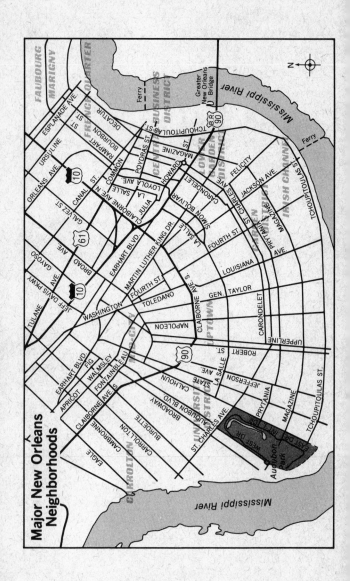

Major New Orleans
Neighborhoods

The French Quarter

The French Quarter—the Quarter—is a historic district, a residential district, and contains some 90 square blocks of jazz clubs, hotels, shops, cafés, and ancient buildings gussied up in frilly ironwork. Also called the Vieux Carre (pronounced *view ka-ráy* and meaning "old square"), the Quarter is actually the old city founded by French Creole settlers in 1718. Its boundaries are the river, North Rampart Street (on the lakeside), Esplanade Avenue (on the downtown side), and Canal Street. Jackson Square is its heartbeat. Surrounded by St. Louis Cathedral, the Cabildo, the Presbytere, and the Pontalba Apartments, all dating back to the city's French and Spanish colonial days, the square is abuzz with artists, tourists, locals, fire-eaters, and tapdancers. On the river side of Jackson Square, the French Market and the Jax Brewery are both shopping extravaganzas located on historic sites, the market having been an Indian trading post, the brewery a brewery. Café du Monde, at the corner of the market, is a 24-hour haven for café au lait and sugary beignets (square-shaped, hole-less doughnuts dusted with powdered sugar; pronounced *ben-yéa*). The ancient flagstones of Pirate's Alley and Pere Antoine's Alley pave the way from the square to Royal Street's art galleries, antique shops, and museums. On nearby Bourbon Street, revelers dressed in cutoffs and carrying paper cups of booze weave in and out of all sorts of bars—topless, bottomless, jazz, gay, historic, and oyster. Music is everywhere, flooding from funky dives, romantic Spanish courtyards, and almost every street corner.

The best way to savor the Quarter's considerable charms is to stroll slowly through it. You can pick up a wealth of free information, including maps, in the New Orleans Welcome Center at 529 St. Ann Street in Jackson Square. Ubiquitous police see to it that the city's primary source of tourist dollars is the safest section of town. However, after dark, Dauphine and Burgundy streets in the lower Quarter are rather desolate; you should stick to the heavily trafficked, well-lighted area around Jackson Square and Royal and Bourbon streets. (And speaking of bourbon, anyone who aims to drink Bourbon Street dry should know that rolling drunks is virtually a cottage industry here.) If you'd rather not go it alone, however, the National Park Rangers conduct free daily walking tours of the Quarter. Call 589–2636 for information, or just stop by their booth at Dumaine and Decatur streets in the French Market. (The Rangers also conduct free tours of the Garden District and the city's oldest above-ground cemetery.) The Friends of the Cabildo tour (fee $5) includes admission to a museum. Their tours begin at the Presbytere every day except Monday at 9:30 A.M. and 1:30 P.M.

At the lakeside border of the Quarter, St. Ann Street leads across the former ramparts of Rampart Street to Armstrong Park. Named for native son Louis Armstrong, the park is on the site of what many believe to have been the real birthplace of jazz—old Congo Square. Perserverance Hall, the old-time jazz hall (not to be confused with Preservation Hall), the Municipal Auditorium, Beauregard Square, and the modern Theatre for the Performing Arts are all in the park. Not far away, a housing project occupies the Basin Street site of the city's old red-light district, notorious Storyville. Right next door are the ancient, white, above-ground tombs and mausoleums of St. Louis Cemetery #1. This area is still a bit notorious. You should not visit this cemetery alone, and if you're in the habit of hanging out in graveyards at night this is not the place to indulge yourself. Take the tour given by the Park Rangers!

Outside the Quarter

The **CBD,** the business district and nerve center of the
port, is bordered by Canal Street, the river, and,
roughly, Loyola and Howard avenues. Second only to
the Quarter in posh lodgings and eateries, the CBD
also has its share of historic buildings and monuments
sprinkled amidst its skyscrapers, motels, churches,
fast-food chains, stores, and convention centers.
Among the historic landmarks in the CBD is Gallier
Hall, a splendid Greek Revival building which was
once city hall for the Americans who settled this area.
The old city hall overlooks New Orleans's second oldest square, Lafayette Square; across the square on
Camp Street is St. Patrick's Church, patterned after
England's York Minister. Other places of interest in
the CBD range from the gray granite Old Customs
House to the Superdome, which looks more like a big
overturned soupbowl than a sports and entertainment
arena. Near the Customs House and the river, Canal
Place is a toney mall featuring the likes of Saks, Gucci,
and Laura Ashley. Alongside the river is the Riverwalk
development, whose specialty shops and eateries
began thriving in 1986. Adjacent to Riverwalk is the
Canal Street Wharf, where riverboats wait to be
boarded, and nearby is the landing for the free ferry.
While the CBD bustles with activity during daylight
hours, it should be noted that the areas around Lafayette Square and the Superdome are best avoided at
night. The Warehouse District, which sprawls along
the Mississippi just upriver from the CBD, should also
be avoided after dark.

Canal Street was once the dividing line between
the French Creoles in the Vieux Carre and the Ameri-
cans who arrived and settled outside of the Quarter.
For that reason, street names change as you cross
Canal from the French Quarter. St. Charles Avenue—
Royal Street on the Quarter side of Canal—is the main

artery through the uptown sections of town, and the St. Charles Streetcar, boarded at Canal Street and Carondelet, is the best introduction to the uptown sights. At Lee Circle, St. Charles Avenue intersects with Howard Avenue, and it is about here that the area known as the **Lower Garden District** begins. Rapidly becoming a yuppie enclave, this old historic district nestles between Howard Avenue and Felicity, Prytania, and Magazine streets. Magazine Street runs parallel to St. Charles through the working class neighborhood of the Irish Channel and eventually runs smack into Audubon Zoo. In between the channel and the zoo, Magazine is an antique seeker's dream. There are a few notable eateries in the channel, but it isn't a good idea to wander around here at night. St. Charles Avenue—the "Avenue"—with its lovely live oaks and deluxe digs, is one of the prettiest streets in town. In some sections of it, neighborhoods on either side—some a mere block away—are seedy and unsafe. But between Louisiana, Jackson, and St. Charles avenues and Magazine Street is the posh, primarily residential **Garden District.** Amidst all this luxury—natural and manmade—are some fine hotels, guesthouses, restaurants, and upscale shopping areas. Further uptown, opposite Tulane and Loyola universities, Audubon Park is 400 acres of greenery and scenery—a fit place indeed for jogging, picnicking, horseback riding, and daydreaming. And the 58-acre Audubon Zoo is a must-do. Many of the neighborhood bars and cafés in the university section are great jazz haunts.

Esplanade Avenue, the downtown border of the Quarter, runs from near the river through Mid-City right to the entrance of City Park. One of the largest parks in the country, City Park's 1,500 acres are graced with lagoons, picnic grounds, and giant live oaks dressed in lacy Spanish moss. The fabled Duelling Oaks (reputed site of many Creole duels) and the white neoclassical building housing the New Orleans Museum of Art are near the park's Esplanade Avenue entrance. Other places of interest in residential Mid-City are the burial grounds of Greenwood and Metairie Cemeteries, and one of the city's two racetracks, the Fairgrounds. The Fairgrounds is also one of the main locations of the annual Jazz & Heritage Festival.

On Lake Pontchartrain, some of the city's best seafood restaurants are in West End Park and the little village of Bucktown. During the long sunny summers locals flock to the lake area for water sports and for picnicking on Lakeshore Drive. Also on the lakefront is the University of New Orleans, whose arena is the site of major concerts and other attractions. The lake area is predominantly residential, with modern homes, concrete shopping centers, and few hotels.

If you want to know what New Orleans is really all about, put on some jeans and ease on down to the French Market on a Saturday or Sunday afternoon. Hang loose in an open-air café, like the Gazebo or the Mediterranean, and listen to some of the city's best musicians blow hot licks and lay down barrelhouse. Regulars show up every weekend—not just "civilians," but other musicians as well, enjoying a busman's holiday. Frilly parasols puncture the air, pumped up and down by second-liners (parade-followers) dancing through the crowd. Hands clap, toes tap, everybody's happy. This is not a show whipped up for tourists, any more than Mardi Gras is. It's just New Orleans, doing what it does best: having a grand old time.

General Information

The character and culture of New Orleans are defined in large part by its subtropical climate. Moisture-laden air and an average annual temperature of about 70 degrees Fahrenheit account for lush banana trees, tall palms, and a veritable Eden of exotic vegetation. Architects everywhere kow-tow to Mother Nature. Here they bow with great flourishes. A heat-shielding gallery doesn't *have* to be graced with dramatic ironwork. And the laid-back tempo of the town is at least partly due to the long, hot, and sultry summers.

Sun-drenched summer peaks during June, July, and August. Temperatures are in the hot-and-sticky 90s for days, even weeks on end. Mercury-matching humidity can make the brilliant blue sky seem like a heavy cloak slung over the city. Things do get sticky here in the summer. Absolutely everything (except Preservation Hall) is air-conditioned, and there is hardly a hotel, restaurant, bar, or bazaar without a ceiling fan whirring away.

New Orleans weather is devilishly unpredictable. Those pretty white ice-cream-cone clouds can abruptly melt and dump rain down like water from an overturned bucket. Summer showers are usually brief pouts, with skies clearing as quickly as the clouds appeared. But summer is also hurricane season. High winds and heavy rains are sometimes the city's taste of a storm tormenting the coastline to the south. It's a dandy idea to bring along an umbrella no matter what time of year you come.

Fall days are warm but usually not scorchers. Eighty degrees in December is not unusual, but the norm by then is about 60. Gray days begin about mid-December and last through late February. Torrents of rain can fall during this period, when the average storm can dump four to five inches on the city. But attacks are usually brief, and even when Mardi Gras falls in early February few parades are ever "called" on account of the weather. And there will be plenty of sunny days as well. One thing to note, however: A mild-sounding 55 degrees can be near bone-chilling, due to the high humidity. With winter temperatures ranging anywhere from 40 to 70 degrees, you may need anything from light cottons to heavy coats and gloves.

A profusion of brilliant azaleas bursts forth in mid-March when things begin to warm up for real. While every man, woman, and child should see Mardi Gras at least once, it's really not recommended for a first visit. Best come first during Spring Fiesta, which begins the first Friday night after Easter with a romantic parade through Jackson Square; this is when the city is at its glorious best. Everything is in bloom, and special fiesta tours take you into places not otherwise open to the public. It's the time to see the secluded courtyards and private homes.

What to Pack

Think of New Orleans as a cosmopolitan tropical resort. Funky jazz dives abound, as do chic hotels and sedate restaurants.

From spring through fall, and sometimes even in winter, New Orleans's street scene features short-shorts, cutoffs, sandals, halters—the least clothing the law allows. Streetwear in the French Quarter is particularly exotic. In a place where people routinely amble about in pirate costumes and Indian head-dresses, hoteliers and restaurateurs have a Romanesque attitude toward dress and decorum. They have seen many things.

Whatever time of year you choose to visit, you should bring an umbrella, sunglasses, a swimsuit (with sandals and a robe suitable for flapping through the hotel lobby), short-sleeved clothing, the most comfortable walking shoes you have (Topsiders or such for riverboats, and ladies, a scarf for the breezy river), and the most casual sightseeing gear you feel comfortable wearing. Ladies should bring one or two dresses for chic places, and perhaps something with spaghetti straps for supper-clubbing. Men will need a jacket and tie for many of the restaurants. Speaking of which, rich Creole and Cajun food is one of the city's trademarks. Clothes with expandable waistlines will feel very comfortable indeed.

Don't buy anything new for summertime sightseeing here. Your crisp new things will quickly wilt in the heat. Bring the coolest, most comfortable things you own for your daytime activities. Ladies' dining-out clothes can be cotton sundresses. Men's jackets and slacks should be very lightweight.

You can cover all bases in unpredictable winter with a sweater or wind-breaker and a heavy raincoat—one with a zip-out lining would be ideal. Bring a pull-over sweater and a couple of T-shirts for daytime carousing. You may wear one T-shirt at a time, or both of them underneath the pullover. While days can be in the balmy 60s, winter nights are usually chilly. Ladies might pack a wool suit with one or two blouses, or a lightweight long-sleeved wool dress. Men will get by fine in a lightweight wool blazer and slacks. (If you come during Mardi Gras, unless you have local connections you can leave your ball gowns and tuxedos at home. The public parades lead to invitation-only balls.)

If you bring a tote bag with shoulder straps for your camera, film, guidebooks, souvenirs, etc., your hands will be free for ice-cream cones and beignets.

Getting There

You can arrive in New Orleans by land, by air, or via the most romantic route in the country: the Mississippi River.

If you arrive by air, your plane will land at New Orleans International Airport, which is served by all major domestic airlines, several commuter lines, and a few international carriers. The airport is about 15 miles west of New Orleans, in Kenner, a 20 to 30 minutes ride from the French Quarter and the CBD. Cab rates into the city are $18 for the first three passengers, $6 for each additional person. The blue-and-white Orleans Transportation vans can be boarded under the Airport Limousine sign just outside the terminal. One way per-person fare is $7, and the vans stop at all the hotels and guesthouses. For 65 cents you can take a city bus from the airport to the CBD, but the bus makes frequent stops and the trip takes at least an hour.

A car may be rented at the airport, but if you're staying in the French Quarter or the CBD you won't need one. Cabs are plentiful, and the rate of $1.10 drop, $1 per mile beats the hassle of a car. Many of the areas described in this book are easily accessible by bus or streetcar and are best explored on foot. A car will come in handy for excursions outside the city and can be rented easily when the time comes. Ask at your hotel, comparison-shop the many rental agencies, or check local newspapers for special two- and three-day rates.

Interstate 10 strings across the southern United States all the way from Florida, through downtown New Orleans, and on to California. Lake Michigan connects with Lake Pontchartrain via Interstate 55, and Interstate 59 is the line to the northeast. U.S. Highways 61 and 90 also run through the city.

If you do plan to drive in the city, there are several things you should be aware of. While almost all of the hotels in New Orleans have some sort of parking facilities, there is usually a $4 to $7 daily fee. In only a few is the parking free. In the Quarter, streets are narrow (many of them have been blocked-off and turned into pedestrian malls), traffic is awesome, especially on weekends and during the frequent special events, and parking signs can be baffling. The city issues parking permits to Quarter residents and business people, whose cars are marked by windshield stickers. Because of traffic congestion and the obvious danger of blocked fire hydrants in this old historic district, French Quarter police play hard-ball when it comes to parking violations, and unstickered cars are often towed away—fast. If your car is towed away it will cost you $100 to get it back, not counting the aspirin. During Mardi Gras there is a $100 fine for blocking a parade route, so if you're driving around during Carnival you'd best know where the parades are. It's much better to put your car in a secured garage and leave it until you need it for out-of-town sightseeing. If your hotel does not have parking facilities, try one of these 24-hour garages: Downtown Parking Service (529–5708), with more than 70 garages throughout the city charging from $5 to $7 for 24 hours; Metropolitan Garage (716 Iberville in the Quarter) and at Poydras Plaza Parking (639 Poydras in the CBD), each with

24-hour parking for about $8. All-day parking in most garages is about $4.

There is direct service to New Orleans via Amtrak trains from New York, Chicago, and Los Angeles. Call 800–USA–RAIL for information about fare and schedules from your city.

New Orleans is also served by Greyhound and Trailways buses. As of now neither has a toll-free number, but you can call the local number for nationwide route information.

Of all the ways to get to New Orleans, steamboating on the mighty Mississippi River is *the* way to travel down to Nostalgia, USA. Three luxury paddlewheelers plough downriver from northern ports at a 19th-century speed of nine miles per hour, calling at river cities along the way. Dixieland bands, banjos, straw boaters and garters, mint juleps, delicate verandahs, and posh staterooms—all can be found on a vessel that looks like a gussied-up wedding cake. The trip is not cheap, nor is it fast. But if you've ample time, and a fairly plump purse, you can treat yourself to a trip you'll daydream about for the rest of your life. The grand old dowager *Delta Queen* and her sister ship the *Mississippi Queen* are operated by the Delta Queen Steamboat Company (800–543–1949). The super-elegant *New Orleans* of American Cruise Lines was christened in July 1985 (phone 504–522–4425). *Bon voyage!*

Getting Around

Everything about New Orleans is easy-going, including getting around town. The Regional Transit Authority's excellent bus system covers the city and includes shuttle buses in both the business district and the French Quarter. The CBD shuttle runs through the business district to and from the Superdome, with clearly marked stops along the way. The French Quarter mini-bus, which looks like a miniature trolley, runs through the Quarter to the foot of Canal Street.

For many locals, one of the city's historic landmarks is also the easiest way to get from uptown home to CBD office. For visitors, the St. Charles Streetcar, also operated by the RTA, is a giddy sightseeing excursion. The streetcar can be boarded at Canal and Carondelet, and runs all the way up St. Charles to Claiborne. Along the way it rumbles and clangs through the Garden District, past Tulane and Loyola university campuses, Audubon Park and the Zoo. A round-trip ride covers about 13 miles and takes about an hour and a half. Note: you'll have to pay another fare for the return trip. A little tip: the street markers along St. Charles are in the center of the neutral ground (or median) on which the streetcar runs, and are more easily read from either the front of the car or from the back (where you can clearly see what you've just passed).

Fare for all buses (except the CBD shuttle, which is 30 cents) and the streetcar is 60 cents, exact change, with five cents extra for a transfer.

The RTA also puts out an easy-to-read, color-coded route map, which can be obtained free at tourist center locations listed at the end of this chapter. There is also a 24-hour information center at 569–2700 (569–2838 for the hearing impaired).

The free ferry, boarded at the landing at the foot of Canal Street, runs back and forth across the Mississippi between the CBD and Algiers, on the West Bank. It's a delightful way to see the city and the river. A round-trip takes about 25 minutes. You can get off and have lunch or dinner in Algiers, or stay on the ferry and come right back.

Local Lexicon

Of course, the official language here is English. But there are some colloquialisms which can be baffling:

Creoles were the original French settlers. The term is now used to describe almost anything indigenous to this area, from a person to a tomato.

Cajuns, also French, are descendants of the Acadians who migrated to southwestern Louisiana from Nova Scotia in the 18th century.

(Creole and Cajun cuisine—America's only regional cuisine—is described in the *Dining* section of this book.)

Neutral ground is a median down the center of a boulevard.

Lagniappe (*lán-yap*) is a bonus, a nice little unexpected something.

a **Banquette** (*bán-ket*) is a sidewalk.

Beignets (*ben-yéas*) are hot, square-shaped, holeless doughnuts sprinkled with powdered sugar.

Gris-gris (*grée-gree*) is a voodoo charm or curse.

Mardi Gras (French for Fat Tuesday) is Carnival, the big two-week celebration just before Ash Wednesday and the beginning of Lent.

Krewes (*crews*) are social organizations which celebrate Carnival with elaborate parades and balls.

Doubloons (*dub-loóns*) are much-coveted "coins" tossed by the masked krewe members from their floats during a parade.

Pralines (*práh-leens*) are rich candy patties made with sugar, butter, and pecans.

Second-liners are parade followers. The term derives from jazz funerals, when mourners fall in line behind the jazz band, singing and dancing and twirling parasols in a great celebration of the release of the soul of the departed.

Locals also have cantankerous ways of pronouncing street names. Notably, **Conti** (*cón-tie*), **Chartres** (*chár-ters*), **Carondelet** (the accent is on the second syllable and the last syllable is pronounced "let"), **Iberville** (*eye-berville*), **Terpsichore** (*turp-see-core*), **Calliope** (the accent is on the first syllable, which rhymes with "pal"), **Burgundy** (the accent is on the middle syllable), **Clio** (*ca-líe-o*), **Milan** (*my-lan*), and **Melpomene** (*mél-po-meen*). **Tchoupitoulas** is perfectly obvious (*Chop-a-tóo-lus*).

Nice to Know

New Orleans is in the Central time zone, one hour behind Eastern time. The telephone area code is 504. For information dial 1–411, and in case of emergency dial 911.

The Greater New Orleans Tourist & Convention Commission can be very helpful in planning your trip. Write to them at 1520 Sugar Bowl Drive, New Orleans, Louisiana 70112, or call 504–566–5068 for maps, brochures, and information about lodging and special events in this eventful city. The Tourist Commission also staffs a desk at the New Orleans International Airport, near the Customs area, and at 334 Royal Street. The New Orleans Welcome Center, at 529 St. Ann Street on Jackson Square, is full of free information. It's open from 10 A.M. until 6 P.M. every day except Monday.

The current New Orleans sales tax is nine percent, and the hotel tax is 11 percent.

Tours

A great way to see the city and its environs is in the small vans of **Inter-Tour-Louisiane** (call 367–3963). The tours are conducted with great enthusiasm by a transplanted Frenchwoman (whose English, incidentally, is flawless). A three-hour city tour is $20; the six and one-half-hour bayou tour is $40; and the $50 plantation tour, with lunch at Nottoway included in the price, is a special treat. All tours include hotel pick-up.

Grey Line (525–0138) also offers several options. You can tour the town for $16, see "New Orleans After Dark" for $32, or view the plantations for $30. In the latter instance, the price does not include lunch. Hotel pick-up is included.

All proceeds from **An Architectural Tour of the CBD** go to the Preservation Resource Center, which conducts tours that leave every Tuesday and Thursday at 9:30 A.M. from the concierge desk at the Hotel Inter-Continental. Cost is $6, and you'll need a reservation (581–7032).

How about tooling down to Nottoway in a white, chauffeur-driven Rolls Royce Silver Cloud? Lazing about on lush grounds and feasting on a catered picnic complete with white linen napery? It is all but a phone call and about $500 away (depending upon the itinerary and the eats). Simply call **London Livery, Ltd.** at 944–1984. The same folks can also arrange for you and 40 or 50 of your friends to board a sleek 65-foot yacht and go for a mini-cruise on Lake Pontchartrain. The $750 for the three-hour party includes captain, crew, and cocktails.

The **New Orleans Rudder Club** (282–2472) will sail you around the lake for three or four hours at $25 per person (minimum eight people). Their Coast Guard-licensed 46-foot ketch is outfitted with full gallery, two baths, etc.

If you've ever wanted to fish the deep waters of the Gulf of Mexico, there are several ways to fulfill your fantasy. Among them is the 65-foot *Miss Mississippi*, which sails out of Empire, about 65 miles from New Orleans on Highway 23. She'll take you out for a full day of fishing each Wednesday through Sunday in the summertime, and the $33 cost per person includes equipment and ice for your hamper. Call Mondays at 9 A.M. to make a reservation (282–8111).

There's no better way to see South Louisiana's beautiful cypress swamps than under the guidance of ecologist Dr. Paul Wagner. His flatboats take you for a natural high into the heart of Honey Island Swamp, one of North America's least altered wetlands. A two-hour tour costs $17.50 ($10 for kids under 12). If you haven't got a car, a van will pick you up at your hotel and deliver you to the Wagner's home in Slidell, from which the tours depart. The $40 fare includes the swamp tour. You can also arrange for hunting and fishing expeditions. Call Dr. Wagner at 641–1769.

And if you find that you can't leave the special sounds of the city behind, take home a "talking scrapbook" called *Your Sound Promenade*. The audio walking tour of the Quarter is recorded on two 90-minute cassettes, and the $19.95 package includes a map. It can be purchased in New Orleans at B. Dalton Bookstores, or call the Promenade at 282–1932 for information.

Hotels

In New Orleans, every hotel is air-conditioned, virtually all have swimming pools, and most boast a courtyard. Except where noted, expect a phone, color television, and private bath. There are a few European-style guesthouses which have none of these, however.

Most hotels and some guesthouses offer attractive

packages during the year. Ask about special rates when you call to reserve. Remember, too, that offerings in many hotels may run the gamut from bargain packages in summer (when temperatures soar) to luxury suites costing hundreds—even thousands—of dollars a day. Rates in every hotel vary according to season. Rooms are always at a premium for the Sugar Bowl, Mardi Gras, and the Jazz Fest. Savvy visitors know to book about a year in advance of the most popular events, and when New Orleans hosts the Super Bowl . . . well, jot this down: the next Super Bowl game will be played here on January 28, 1990. And Mardi Gras falls on March 3, 1987, and on February 16, 1988.

Price categories listed for hotels are as follows: over $150 is *Expensive;* $90–$150 is *Moderate;* and under $90 is *Inexpensive.* Categories are approximate, and except where noted, are based on double occupancy.

Regardless of the time of year you come, *make sure you understand the cancellation policy of your hotel.* Also, many hotels require a three- or four-day minimum during special events, and you may be asked to make full payment in advance.

Depending upon the hotel, there is a charge of from $7 to $20 for an extra person in the room, except for children sharing a room with parents. In the latter case, the sharing child can be anywhere from under 12 to under 20, depending upon the policy of the hotel.

The French Quarter

In the 1880s Mark Twain summed up a lyrical piece on the French Quarter as follows: "This charming decoration cannot be successfully imitated; nor is it to be found elsewhere in America." In the 1980s, a tourist, gaping down Bourbon Street and taking swigs from a paper cup of booze, was overheard saying, "Aw, man, I never saw anything like this in my life."

It looks like the set for a romantic epic motion picture. Quaint pastel buildings, few taller than three stories, are garnished with "gingerbread" or ornate cast-iron. Flagstone carriageways sweep from narrow streets to courtyards with tiered fountains and tropical greenery. Lush plants dangle from virtually every eave. Delighted epicures, historians, boozers, jazz aficionados, voodoo cultists, honeymooners, costumed kooks, and collectors of everything wander in and out of carefully preserved 18th- and 19th-century structures, encountering on nearly every corner the exotic legends of Jean Lafitte and Marie Laveau. Many of the Quarter's 7,000 or so somewhat smug residents see no reason ever to venture beyond its borders.

Designed by French engineers in 1721, the Old Square is actually a rectangle, 13 blocks long and six blocks deep, with streets laid out in a perfect grid.

The heaviest tourist traffic is in Jackson Square, and on Bourbon, Royal, and Chartres between the square and Canal Street. That area has the greatest concentration of hotels, most of the famous restaurants, and much—but not all—of that jazz. The lower Quarter, from St. Ann to Esplanade, is predominantly residential and gay. But there are also hotels (a couple of stunning ones), a few good cafés, and several interesting historical sights.

The centerpiece of the original colony was the Place d'Armes, or parade grounds. Renamed for the hero of the Battle of New Orleans, **Jackson Square** is still the heartbeat of the Quarter. It's a pedestrian mall, with Chartres, St. Peter, St. Ann, and Decatur framing an ongoing scene of dixieland bands, tap dancers, mimes, curious tourists, and nonchalant locals. At the **New Orleans Welcome Center,** 529 St. Ann, you can get a wealth of information and helpful advice, all at no charge.

In the middle of the square, the old parade ground is a pretty landscaped park. Shade trees, shrubs, and park benches encircle a colossal statue of Andrew Jackson. The park's fence is decorated with paintings by the artists who work in the square, unfazed by the clowns, the music, and the movement. Forming an ethereal backdrop for the earthy scene are **St. Louis Cathedral,** the **Cabildo** and the **Presbytere** on Chartres, and the twin **Pontalba Buildings,** with their almost lyrical cast-iron facades, which line St. Peter and St. Ann.

Free guided tours of the country's oldest cathedral are conducted daily, except during services. (Mass is sometimes accompanied by the beat of a bongo or the low moan of a saxophone in the Square.) History buffs love browsing through the historical documents in the Cabildo and Presbytere. The Louisiana Purchase agreement was signed on the second floor of the Cabildo, which once held colonial government offices. Here you can also see a death mask of Napoleon. The Cabildo and Presbytere museums are open daily except Monday from 10 A.M. to 6 P.M. Admission to each is $2. Another museum in the Square is on St. Ann in the "lower Pontalbas." At the **1850 House,** you can see what upscale life was like in the mid-19th century. The tri-level restored apartments contain period furnishings and meticulous details. Hours and admission are the same as the other two museums.

(For all hotels and attractions, credit card abbreviations are as follows: AE, American Express; CB, Carte Blanche; DC, Diners Club; MC, Master Card; V, Visa. "All major credit cards" means that all of these cards will be accepted).

Kids will get a kick out of the **Pontalba Historical Puppetorium** on St. Peter. Puppets and dolls are sold in the front of the shop, and in the Puppet Museum an automated show colorfully depicts the Battle of New Orleans (open daily 9:30 A.M. to 6 P.M.; adults $2, kids $1). And everybody will enjoy St. Ann Street, which is sweet-tooth city. **La Madeleine** bakes its croissants and pastries daily. Next door is the **Chocolate Chip Cookie Company. Creole Delicacies** has a variety of goodies, including homemade pralines which you can sample from a basket on the counter. **Angelo Brocato's** is an 80-year gelateria, famous for its spumoni and cannoli. And if you want a full meal in an informal setting, the **Jackson Square Café** on the corner is operated by the Guste family, owners of Antoine's. Its burgers, salads, and Creole dishes cost from $3–$12 (801 Decatur Street; 504–523–5061; all major credit cards). Across Decatur, **Café du Monde** is *the* place for beignets and café au lait. Open around the clock, and a great people-watching spot, this open-air café has been a local favorite for more than a century.

Decatur is always lined with colorful carriages drawn by horses or mules in silly hats and flowers. A carriage tour is a fun way to see the Quarter, with guides dispensing enthusiastic fact and fiction about the old colony. Half-hour rides are $7 per person.

Pretty **Washington Artillery Park** across from the square is a popular spot for viewing the square and the river. Mimes and musicians often take to the promenade to entertain the congregation of locals and tourists. You can get an even better look at the river across the railroad tracks on **Moon Walk.** You can park on a bench, munch the muffuletta you picked up at the Central Grocery Co., and watch Old Man River just keep rolling along.

In the late 17th century, Choctaws and Chickasaws traded with French and Spanish explorers on the banks of the river. That site has been a marketplace since early colonial days. A $3.2 million renovation in 1975 produced the present **French Market,** stretched out behind Café du Monde. Shops, icecream parlors, and cafés lace through the colonnades and arcades. It's *the* place to be on weekend afternoons. The **Mediterranean Café** (1000 Decatur; 504–523–2302; AE) serves inexpensive souvlaki, pizza, and dixieland; the nearby **Gazebo** (1018 Decatur; 504–522–0862; AE, MC, V) specializes in salads, seafood, and dixieland; free jazz concerts are the highlight at **Dutch Alley.** These are all great places to hear jazz, watch the second-liners, or join in the fun. And if chess is your game, you'll find several challengers with boards at the ready.

And speaking of jazz, it almost goes through the roofs of those quaint old buildings on Bourbon Street. There's just no place quite like Bourbon. It's great fun just strolling down it, listening to the jazz and the wise-cracking barkers, and watching the tap dancers, costumed characters, and clowns. "The Street" is a mixed bag of the seedy and the chic. Sedate Galatoire's is right there, as are tacky topless and bottomless bars. Two time-worn institutes of higher imbibing are the **Absinthe House Bar,** at #238, and the **Old Absinthe House,** at #400, both of which display plaques attesting to the authenticity of their claims that Jean Lafitte and Andrew Jackson conspired within their ancient walls.

The deluxe **Royal Sonesta Hotel** manages to be a peaceful oasis for its guests while at the same time housing some of the liveliest bars and restaurants on the Street—the Mystick Den, Le Boozé Bars, Desire Oyster Bar, Begue's Lounge, and the chic Begue's Restaurant. Above its cool white marble lobby and crystal chandeliers are French country-style rooms in pastels and prints. Everyone's bed is turned down, but the privileged check into the private-access Tower for its considerable advantages. Moderate. (300 Bourbon Street, New Orleans 70140; 504–586–0300 or 800–343–7170; all major credit cards) 1 800-7663782

The **Landmark Bourbon Street Hotel** occupies one of the busiest (read noisiest) corners in the Quarter. Its 186 identical Williamsburg-style rooms have double or king-sized beds, which you'll only gaze at longingly if you take a room with a balcony overlooking Bourbon. Two floors have public balconies, from which you can watch the street's scenes and then retire to a quiet room on the back for some sleep. The hotel has wheelchair ramps, Braille elevators, and an entire floor for nonsmokers. Its cafés, cabarets, and lounges are lively spots. Moderate. (541 Bourbon Street, New Orleans 70130; 504–524–7611 or 800–535–7891; all major credit cards)

Bourbon is but a block away from the **Olivier House Hotel,** a small jewel more like a private home than a guest house. Many of the 40 rooms have balconies, kitchenettes, or working fireplaces, and all are furnished with antiques. The French doors of #103 and #107 open onto the secluded pool area in one of three lavish courtyards. There are split-levels and elegant suites, as well as budget accommodations. Foreigners and theatrical people are fond of the hotel, which often houses the entire cast and crew of a touring show playing the Saenger. Inexpensive. (828 Toulouse Street, New Orleans 70112; 504–525–8456; AE, DC, MC, V)

In the 700 block of Royal, Pere Antoine's and Pirate's Alleys lead to Jackson Square, cutting alongside St. Anthony's Garden and the Cathedral. Both alleys were cut in 1831, long after Jean Lafitte and company had disappeared. Nevertheless, the legend persists that Andrew Jackson and Lafitte conspired here to plan the Battle of New Orleans. Facts notwithstanding, there are few places more redolent of the city's exotic history than those cracked passageways.

A few steps from St. Anthony's Garden, those huge white paneled doors on Orleans Street open into the **Bourbon Orleans.** Guests help themselves to apples in the white marbled lobby Promenade and dine in pretty Café Lafayette. The 200 French country-style rooms are furnished with Chippendale and Queen Anne; pink marble baths have not only phones but televisions as well. Among many amenities are turn-down service, electric clock radios, and, for business travelers, an office-away-from-the-office and complimentary limousine service to the CBD. Moderate. (717 Orleans, New Orleans 70116; 504–523–2222 or 800–521–5338; all major credit cards)

On St. Ann across from the Presbytere, the **Place d'Armes Hotel's** 74 rooms are in eight adjoining slave quarter and row houses dating from 1790. Rooms have one or two double beds, and some have balconies overlooking Jackson Square. However, there are rooms in the hotel which have no windows—check that out before you check in. Guests gather for complimentary continental breakfast in a pretty white brick room overlooking a stunning courtyard. Inexpensive. (625 St. Ann, New Orleans 70116; 504–524–4531 or 800–535–7791; AE, DC, MC, V)

There are changing exhibits in the first-floor Williams Gallery of the **Historic New Orleans Collection,** and ten other galleries containing maps and documents pertaining to the city's rich past. Historians flock to its excellent research library. The Williams Gallery is free and open to the public, and for $2 you can tour the rest of the place. The perfectly restored house was built in 1792, and the stories about it are worth the two bucks. It's open Tuesday through Saturday from 10 A.M. to 4:30 P.M. (533 Royal Street, New Orleans 70130; 504–523–4662)

An exquisite etched-glass door lets you into the **Maison de Ville,** a totally captivating 15-room European-style hotel. (Long-time resident Tennessee Williams lived in #9 in the attached slave quarters.) Soothing earth tones, pastel prints, marble basins with brass fittings, king, queen, or double 18th-century four-posters, turndown service, and breakfast served on a silver tray are among its pleasures. Splendid though it is, life in the main house is tough compared to that in the hotel's cottages on nearby Dauphine Street. Want your own French Quarter cottage and private patio? Pool surrounded by landscaped grounds and marble statuary? Concierge to cater to your every whim? Such is life in the Audubon Cottages —named for naturalist John J., who lived in Cottage #1 in 1821. Singles, doubles, suites, and cottages. Expensive. (727 Toulouse Street, New Orleans 70130; 504–561–5858 or 800–634–1600; AE, MC, V)

And speaking of the playwright, the **Tennessee Williams Walk** takes you on a stroll to about 40 places in which he lived, ate, drank, and worked. The two-hour guided tour costs $15 per person. Tour by appointment, 504–566–7592.

The old St. Louis Hotel caused quite a stir when it opened in the mid-19th century. So did the **Royal Orleans** when its doors opened on the same site in 1960. If you're not willing to let loose of $130 for a single, skip ahead. There are acres of marbled lobby, priceless statuary, polished brass, and 356 rooms graced with custom-made furnishings and original artwork. Each sumptuous suite is in a different decor, with phones and other frills (sometimes jacuzzis!) in marble baths. You can dine in pretty pink Café Royale or the Rib Room (see *Dining*), and snack and swim at the rooftop La Riviera. Even if you're not staying here, stop in for flaming coffee and French pastries in the plush Esplanade Lounge just off the lobby. Expensive. (621 St. Louis, New Orleans 70140; 504–529–5333 or, since the R.O. is an Omni Classic Hotel, 800–THE–OMNI; all major credit cards)

From the Royal Orleans, you'll stroll past Antoine's (713 St. Louis) in order to reach the **Hermann-Grima House** at 820 St. Louis, where you can see Creole cooking demonstrations every Thursday between October and May. This American-style brick house was built in 1831 and is on the National Register of Historic Places. It's a lovely, rambling old place, and the separate kitchen in the back is filled with fascinating things. You can tour the house every day except Sunday from 10 A.M. to 3:30 P.M.; $3 for adults, $2 for senior citizens.

The 600-room **Monteleone** is the grande dame of French Quarter hotels. A fourth generation of Monteleones operates the hotel, which celebrates its 100th birthday in 1986. Each guest arriving during the centennial year will receive a complimentary drink in one of the several lounges, and can take part in the various festivities planned for the year. The slowly revolving red-and-white canopied bar of the Carousel Lounge just off the lobby is a landmark meeting place (don't miss it!), and the Aftdeck's oysters on the half-shell are perhaps the best in town. Business, leisure, and celebrity guests flock to this venerable favorite—Paul Newman and Robert Mitchum are among those who've strolled beneath those glittering chandeliers. Rooms are extra-large and cushy, and service is swift and efficient. Pool, Skylight Lounge, and the Duchess Room (with live entertainment) are all on the roof; the concierge is in the lobby. Moderate. (214 Royal Street, New Orleans 70130; 504–523–3341 or 800–535–9595; all major credit cards)

The **St. Louis Hotel** boasts two elegant restaurants behind its cream-colored frilly-ironwork facade —the Savoir Faire and the Louis XVI. The centerpiece of the lobby is a plush rose velvet pouf, and the luxurious courtyard boasts a lovely marble fountain. Second-floor rooms open onto the gallery surrounding that pretty sight, and all rooms are furnished with antiques and either double, twin, king-, or queen-sized beds. Bedside remotes control the televisions; most baths have phone extensions. Moderate. (730 Bienville, New Orleans 70130; 504–581–7300 or 800–535–9111; all major credit cards)

Just up the street at 813 Bienville, **Arnaud's Grill** is a pleasant place to stop in for a drink. There's a long wooden bar, mosaic tile floors, whirring ceiling fans, and an old-time player piano making soothing sounds. Upstairs there's a free exhibit of Mardi Gras gowns worn by Germaine Wells, daughter of the restaurant's founder. (Arnaud's details are in *Dining*.)

The **Musée Conti Museum of Wax** (917 Conti Street) is a lot of fun. Its 31 tableaux are not only well-executed, they're historically accurate as well. Scenes depict the city's history all the way back to 1682, when LaSalle followed the Great River down to its mouth. Costumes are lavish, and some of the faces are startling. The museum is open every day except Mardi Gras and Christmas, from 10 A.M. until 5:30 P.M. Admission is $3, with discounts for senior citizens, students, and kids.

Some of the 50 rooms in the **Prince Conti** are contemporary in design; others are extravagant period affairs with carved antiques, scarlet drapes, and dramatic mirrored walls. (The bath of #248 even has a bidet.) Free valet parking and complimentary continental breakfast are among its niceties. Moderate. (830 Conti Street, New Orleans 70112; 504–529–4172 or 800–535–9706; all major credit cards)

Among the amenities in the **Dauphine Orleans** are free on-premises parking, turn-down service (with a "goodnight treat"), complimentary welcome cocktail and breakfast, in-room movies, and transportation within the Quarter. Suites of the 110-room hotel are in historic buildings off the patio, and if you select #111 you'll be "licensed" to stay in a former bordello. Guests in the "Madam's Room" are issued a copy of the license issued by the city in 1857 to the "lewd and abandoned women" who occupied this site. Other rooms and suites have either modern or period furnishings, king- or queen-sized beds. Moderate. (415 Dauphine Street, New Orleans 70112; 504–586–1800, in Los Angeles, 800–521–6111, elsewhere 800–521–7111; all major credit cards)

The **Holiday Inn's Chateau LeMoyne** adapts beautifully to its French Quarter site. All of the inn's familiar features are here, along with courtyards, iron-filigree balconies, and other Crescent City touches. An expense account crowd mingles with families grateful for a "known" in the wilds of the bawdy Vieux Carre. (There are several Holiday Inns in the city—one on Royal Street and another, the Crowne Plaza, in the CBD.) Parking is free for overnight guests. Moderate. (301 Dauphine Street, New Orleans 70112; 504–581–1303; all major credit cards)

The pretty, multi-balconied **Maison Dupuy's** glorious Fountain of the Arts courtyard boasts a tiered fountain which looks like a huge white wedding cake, and this hotel's guest list has included Elizabeth Taylor, Johnny Carson, and Shirley MacLaine. The French country-style rooms all have king-sized or two double beds, dining is done in Le Bon Creole, and the live entertainment is in Cabaret Lautrec. Inexpensive.

(1001 Toulouse, New Orleans 70112; 504–586–8000
or 800–535–9177; all major credit cards)

Iberville Street, though rather drab, boasts a
number of conveniences. On it are two New Orleans-
flavored Woolworth's (at Rampart and at Bourbon), a
Walgreen's Drugstore (at Royal), and a post office
(between Burgundy and Rampart).

Midway between Jackson Square and Canal, the
Bienville House Hotel is a rather homey place, and its
rooms have carpeting, wallpaper, vanities, and king-
sized or two double beds. (#357 has a carved walnut
canopy bed only slightly smaller than Lake Pontchartrain.) The Pump Room has a sing-along bar, the
courtyard has a pool, and the Bull's Corner has steaks
and other nice things. Inexpensive. (320 Decatur
Street, New Orleans 70130; 504–529–2345 or 800–
535–7836; AE, V)

Don't miss the **Napoleon House,** at 500 Chartres.
It may look like it's about to collapse, but it's one of
the most popular bars in the Quarter. Loaded with
atmosphere, it dates back to about 1797 and was the
19th-century home of Mayor Nicholas Girod. When
Napoleon was exiled on St. Helena, a group of local
admirers, led by Girod, planned to dispatch a rescue
ship for him, captained by one of Jean Lafitte's men,
the dashing Dominique You. The plan expired with
the emperor, but the Napoleon House lives on.
(There's more about it in *Dining*.)

The **Historic Pharmacy Museum,** 514 Chartres,
is an appropriately musty old place which was a drugstore in 1823. There's a 100-year-old leech jar (sorry,
not for sale—you'll have to keep those leeches some-
place else), hand-blown apothecary tubes, bottles,
jars, and a marvelous marble soda fountain, circa
1850. This step back in time will set you back two bits;
open Tuesday through Saturday, 10 A.M. to 5:30 P.M.

Chez Helene, queen of the soul-food restaurants,
recently opened a branch in the plush **Hotel de la
Poste.** A luxury motel, the de la Poste has large, fairly
stylish rooms with king-sized or two double beds, hi-fi,
and AM/FM radios. Posh suites are in slave quarters

with balconies overlooking a magnificent courtyard. The Bacchus Den is a hot spot for cocktails, the pool a pleasant cooling-off place. Moderate. (316 Chartres Street, New Orleans 70130; 504–581–1200 or 800–448–4927; all major credit cards)

You can get divine French pastries for about $1 each in **La Marquise,** 625 Chartres. Coffee and tea are also served, and you can eat inside or in the rear patio. A very good rest stop! Open daily except Wednesday from 7:30 A.M. until 5:30 P.M.

Costumed docents will guide you through the **Beauregard-Keyes House** at 1113 Chartres. Confederate General P.G.T. Beauregard lived in this house, and many years later it was bought by Frances Parkinson Keyes, author of *River Road, Dinner at Antoine's,* and other novels. An English-style formal garden is adjacent to the house. Admission is $3.

The nearby **Soniat House** is no ordinary hotel. Proprietor Rodney Smith furnished the Creole townhouse with the fine antiques he collected during 25 years of world travel. It is exquisite, with deluxe touches like down pillows, Roger & Gallet soaps, bath salts from Provence, and bathside phones. Some suites have jacuzzis. Breakfast is served on a silver tray, room service is available around the clock, and a limo is on hand daily to whisk you to the CBD. The hotel will pack a picnic for you and turn down your bed at night. There is an honor bar in the courtyard beside the lily pond. Moderate. (1133 Chartres, New Orleans 70116; 504–522–0570; MC, V)

The 24-room **Hotel Villa Convento** is Spanish-flavored and a favorite of foreigners eager to avoid the splashy convention hotels. #305–306 is convenient for families, with a bedroom (with king-sized bed) and staircase leading to a loft with twin beds. Many rooms have balconies, and the courtyard is a nice place to have your complimentary croissants and coffee. Inex-

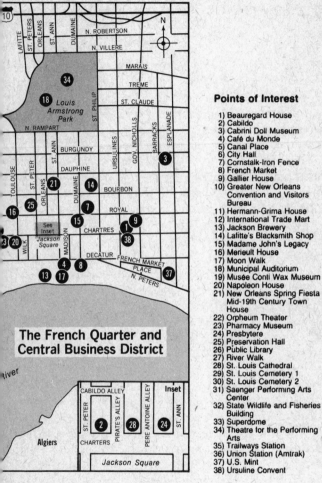

The French Quarter and
Central Business District

Points of Interest

1) Beauregard House
2) Cabildo
3) Cabrini Doll Museum
4) Café du Monde
5) Canal Place
6) City Hall
7) Cornstalk-Iron Fence
8) French Market
9) Gallier House
10) Greater New Orleans
    Convention and Visitors
    Bureau
11) Hermann-Grima House
12) International Trade Mart
13) Jackson Brewery
14) Lafitte's Blacksmith Shop
15) Madame John's Legacy
16) Merieult House
17) Moon Walk
18) Municipal Auditorium
19) Musée Conti Wax Museum
20) Napoleon House
21) New Orleans Spring Fiesta
    Mid-19th Century Town
    House
22) Orpheum Theater
23) Pharmacy Museum
24) Presbytere
25) Preservation Hall
26) Public Library
27) River Walk
28) St. Louis Cathedral
29) St. Louis Cemetery 1
30) St. Louis Cemetery 2
31) Saenger Performing Arts
    Center
32) State Wildlife and Fisheries
    Building
33) Superdome
34) Theatre for the Performing
    Arts
35) Trailways Station
36) Union Station (Amtrak)
37) U.S. Mint
38) Ursuline Convent

pensive. (616 Ursulines Street, New Orleans 70116; 504–522–1793; AE, MC, V)

If you're on a strict budget and willing to forgo croissants, phones, and color television, you won't find a better buy than the **French Quarter Maisonettes**—if you can get in, since it's almost always booked. There are only seven units, and each is a Spartan suite with air-conditioning and private bath. Closed during July. Inexpensive. (1130 Chartres, New Orleans 70116; 504–524–9918; no credit cards)

Another bargain in the lower Quarter is the **Chateau Motel.** Rooms are comfortable and well-kept, and parking is free. The patio bar is tucked under an awning in the courtyard—a pleasant place for breakfast, lunch, or lounging after a dip in the pool. Inexpensive. (1001 Chartres, New Orleans 70116; 504–524–9636; all major credit cards)

Across the street, the **Hotel Provincial** has no fewer than five secluded courtyards and spacious rooms furnished with French antiques. It has a large pool, and on-site parking is free. Its restaurant is the Honfleur (see *Dining*). The hotel is a favorite with senior citizens. Inexpensive. (1024 Chartres, New Orleans 70116; 504–581–4995, in Los Angeles 800–621–5295, elsewhere 800–535–7922; all major credit cards)

Occupying the 400 block of Esplanade, the **Old U. S. Mint** houses two "only in New Orleans" exhibits, both on the second floor. The **Mardi Gras Exhibit** displays elaborate costumes, masks, sceptres, and all sorts of Carnival information. Across the hall, the **Jazz Exhibit** has a collection of instruments played by New Orleans jazzmen, photographs, second-line parasols, one of Satchmo's white handkerchiefs, and other memorabilia pertaining to the city's musical heritage. And parked behind the mint, in mint condition, is a streetcar named Desire—one of the cars from the old Desire streetcar line. Admission of $2 allows you to see the Mardi Gras, the jazz exhibits, and the streetcar daily except Monday, 10 A.M. to 6 P.M.

Across from Esplanade, **A Hotel . . . The French-**

men is a pretty guesthouse behind a rather nonde-
script facade. You'll find high-ceiling rooms, period
furniture, an exercise room, pool, and spa. A special
feature is the *full* complimentary breakfast. How about
pecan waffles and coffee served to you in bed? Standard rooms are small, deluxe rooms have queen-sized
beds, and super-deluxes are huge, with private balconies. Inexpensive. (417 Frenchmen, New Orleans
70116; 504–948–2166 or 800–831–1781; AE, MC, V)

Inside the pink, balconied **Lamothe House** is an
astonishing collection of 19th-century Victorian antiques. It's one of the most opulently furnished hotels
in the Quarter (actually, it's on the fringe of the Quarter). Guests gather for the complimentary *petit déjeuner*
in a formal dining room, where coffee is served from
a 200-year-old Sheffield silver urn. A turned-down
bed is just one of many amenities. Parking is free.
Twenty rooms and nine suites. Moderate. (621 Esplanade, New Orleans 70116; 504–947–1161 or 800–
867–5858; AE, MC, V)

Sneak past the Haunted House at 1140 Royal and
head for the **Gallier House.** Now a museum, the house
was built in about 1858 by famed New Orleans architect James Gallier, Jr. The carefully restored, ele-
gantly furnished old home is probably the most
thoroughly researched historic house in the city. The
formal parlor alone is worth the $3 admission. It is
located at 1132 Royal Street and is open daily except
Sunday from 10 A.M. until 4:30 P.M.

If you're intrigued by tales of Marie Laveau and
her voodoo cult, go to the **Voodoo Museum** at 724
Dumaine. This is not exactly your run of the mill museum. But it does have its . . . charms. In addition to
the gris-gris and occult displays, the museum conducts
a three-and-one-half-hour voodoo tour for $15; if
that's not enough they'll run you out in the swamps to
poke around ghost towns and haunted plantations.

That tour lasts seven and one-half hours and costs $35 (not including a little something for your nerves). Admission to the museum is $3 (students and senior citizens $2, kids $1), and it's open daily from 10 A.M. until 10 P.M. . . . or later.

Just off the foyer of the **Lafitte Guest House** is a lovely Victorian parlor with dramatic scarlet drapes, brass andirons, period furnishings, and rich tapestries. The 14 individually decorated rooms are furnished with fine reproductions and antiques. Many have crystal chandeliers and working fireplaces, and some have balconies. Baths have either shower stalls or tubs. Croissants, orange juice, and coffee are included in the room rate: Moderate. (1003 Bourbon Street, New Orleans 70116; 504–581–2678; AE, MC, V)

Be sure to stop in for a drink at **Lafitte's Blacksmith Shop** across the street at 941 Bourbon. The tattered old cottage, built prior to 1772, is a popular neighborhood bar and has been a favorite of artists and writers, famous and not so, for ages. Everyone loves the (apocryphal) tales of Jean and Pierre Lafitte and the pirates of Barataria who traded smuggled goods here. A great place to soak up atmosphere.

The little 14-room **Cornstalk Hotel** behind the Cornstalk Fence is an elegant inn, and is also on the National Register of Hotels. It's furnished in antiques or reproductions, with a 24-hour staff there to look after things, and the Continental breakfast is included in the room rate. Inexpensive. (915 Royal Street, New Orleans 70116; 504–523–1515; AE, MC, V)

A trim little creole cottage, similar to scores of others in the Quarter, holds the lobby, reception rooms, and restaurant of the neat-as-a-pin **Burgundy Inn.** Diners in Arthur's, the restaurant, gaze out over a tiny but pretty patio and the rambling galleries of the guest cottages. Rooms are immaculate if modest, but the modest prices make this inn a budget traveler's dream come true. Inexpensive. (911 Burgundy Street, New Orleans 70116; 504–524–4401 or 800–535–7785; AE, MC, V)

Beyond the back fence of the inn is the splashy Jazz Garden of the **Landmark French Quarter.** Under the same banner as the Landmark Bourbon, but considerably quieter and somewhat out-of-the-way, the motel offers 100 rooms with double and king-sized beds, free parking, and a restaurant which is open only for breakfast and lunch. An advantage of the rooms on the Rampart Street side is that they overlook Armstrong Park and thus the Mardi Gras parades which wind into Municipal Auditorium for their Carnival balls. It's not the greatest place for bagging beads and doubloons—although some merrymakers have known to try. Inexpensive. (920 Rampart Street, New Orleans 70116; 504–524–3333 or 504–535–7862; all major credit cards)

Looking a bit like a ferris wheel, the broad white arch of **Armstrong Park** spells out the native son's name in blazing lights at night. The park incorporates the site of old Congo Square, where 18th- and 19th-century slaves congregated every Sunday afternoon to chant and dance to drumbeats and bones—African and Caribbean rhythms that still echo today in the music played by jazzmen like Satchmo. Near the Rampart Street entrance is a 12-foot statue of the famous trumpeter, holding his horn and his handkerchief. Wooden bridges criss-cross a winding lagoon, beyond which the jazz complex includes **Perseverance Hall #4** (again, not to be confused with *Preservation* Hall in the Quarter). In about 1820, Perseverance Hall was built as a masonic lodge. Within its walls, and in other music halls around town, early jazzmen blended and fine-tuned the sounds of chants, brass bands, jubilees, and the cries of street vendors into America's great contribution to music. Other buildings in the park are the Theatre for the Performing Arts and Municipal Auditorium. Congo Square, in front of the auditorium, was renamed Beauregard Square in honor of the Confederate general.

"Burials" in New Orleans are done in above-ground tombs for the same reason that there are no subways—you've heard of watery graves? The city's oldest City of the Dead, **St. Louis #1,** is on Basin Street between St. Louis and Conti streets. It was begun in 1788, just after the first conflagration destroyed the colony. Well-worn paths lead past small stark white "houses," ornate miniature Greek temples, and crumbling multiple-crypt vaults. Many of the tombs have ornate grillwork and iron picket fences. Red-dust crosses and gris-gris mark the tomb believed to be the final resting place of Marie Laveau. A crime-ridden housing project is adjacent to this cemetery, and for that reason (and those red-dust crosses) it is not wise to wander about here alone.

On the River

You won't have any trouble locating the *Steamboat Natchez.* Its warbling, off-key calliope alerts everyone in the Western Hemisphere that the riverboat is docked at the Toulouse Street Wharf right behind the Jax Brewery. The 1,600-passenger sternwheeler does daily two-hour narrated harbor cruises, at 11:30 A.M. and at 2:30 P.M. (adults $9.50, children 3–11 $4.75). A dixieland band replaces the narrator on the 6:30 P.M. cruise, and dinner is available at an extra charge. The cruise only is $11.50, but if you want to eat along with the music it's $24 (half-price for children). The 10 P.M.-to-midnight Saturday night dance cruise is $9.50. You can mount the gangplank half an hour before departure time.

The little *Bayou Jean Lafitte* departs at 11 A.M. for its five-hour excursion into the murky reaches of Barataria, once the headquarters of the mysterious brothers Lafitte. There are snack and cocktail bars aboard, so you won't grow faint during the 45-mile voyage. Adults $11.50, half that for kids. This ship also docks at the Toulouse Street Wharf.

The fabulous five-deck sidewheel steamer *President* is an incredible sight to behold. With a capacity of 3,000, the big white floating wedding cake is the largest operating excursion boat on the Mississippi. There are games arcades, a two-deck-high ballroom, live entertainment in the lounge, and, on the top deck, an open-air promenade. The *President* does several cruises, including Sunday Big Band Brunches, weekend moonlight cruises with dinner and dancing, and harbor cruises. Call 504–524–SAIL for info.

The glittering *Creole Queen* paddlewheeler cruises out every night for a Dinner and All That Jazz outing, departing from the Poydras Street Wharf ($26, reservations required; call 504–529–4567). Its twice-daily Plantation River Cruise (10 A.M. and 2 P.M.) includes a one-hour stop at Chalmette so you can explore the site of the bloody Battle of New Orleans, read the inscriptions in the cemetery, and stop in the Beauregard House ($10, half-price for kids).

The $10 "Zoo Cruise" of the *Cotton Blossom* includes round-trip riverboating and admission to Audubon Zoo. But it's also fun to take the St. Charles Streetcar up to the zoo and board the steamboat there for a leisurely drift back downriver. In that event the one-way cruise-only fare is $4.50—$2.25 for the kids.

Outside of the Quarter

The CBD

Adjoining the French Quarter is the Central Business District, known to intimates as the CBD. Within its old cast-iron buildings and modern skyscrapers are foreign consulates, federal and state agencies, the offices of import-export, oil, and gas companies, and control centers for the Port of New Orleans. This is the nation's second largest foreign trade zone. The 15-mile-long port serves about 5,000 foreign vessels annually, with cargo values of about $12 billion.

New Orleans being a major convention city, almost all of the CBD's high-tech high-rise hotels are geared in that direction, and toward anyone whose idea of "quaint" is any place lacking Nautilus equipment. Every hotel in town advertises its close proximity to the city's main attraction, the French Quarter ("a short five-minute stroll," "a mere five miles," etc.), and most hotels go to great lengths to appear as French Quarterly as possible. CBD nightlife is exclusively in the splashy hotel clubs, all of which try to lure tourists away from the Quarter with a great deal of razzle-dazzle.

In the early days, plans had been made to dig a drainage canal along a broad strip of land on the upriver border of the Quarter. The Americans who poured into town in the early 19th century settled in Faubourg Ste. Marie, a former plantation on the upriver side of the intended canal. Thus, the canal was never built, and the strip of land became the "neutral ground" between the Americans and the Creoles, who didn't exactly hit it off. Faubourg Ste. Marie is now the CBD, the proposed canal is Canal Street, and medians are still called neutral grounds. Because Canal was the border of the American Sector, street names change as you cross it from the Vieux Carre—Bourbon to Carondelet, Royal to St. Charles, and so forth.

You can get a great view of the former faubourg and the Quarter from the **free ferry.** The landing is at the foot of Canal and the ferry carries cars as well as people. It leaves every 30 minutes and the crossing to Algiers takes only about 5 minutes—25 if you stay on it and come right back.

If you'd like to watch Carnival in the making, get off the ferry in Algiers, turn right as you leave the landing, and follow the levee until you see the warehouses and sign of **Blaine Kern's Mardi Gras World.** (It's a short walk, and safe in the daytime.) Kern is one of the major float-builders, and many of Carnival's spectacular floats are created in this Santa's workshop in Algiers. You can watch props being made for the greatest free show on earth Monday through Friday, 10 A.M. to 5 P.M.; telephone 504–362–8211. Admission is $2.

The rambling gray structure clutching the levee to the left of the ferry is **Algiers Landing.** The multilevel restaurant serves everything from club sandwiches to crawfish étouffée, and its big plate-glass windows provide a great view of the city and the Quarter. It is especially romantic at night with the skyline lit up and riverboats shining along the river. Meals cost about $30 for two. Telephone 504–362–2981; all major credit cards.

Adjacent to the CBD ferry landing is the International Trade Mart, with the Viewpoint observation deck (open daily from 9 A.M. until 11 P.M.; 504–525–2185), and, on the 33rd floor, the revolving cocktail lounge **Top of the Mart**—a nice way to ride around town. It's open daily, no food is served, and there's usually a one-drink minimum. (An inexpensive cafeteria is on the third floor.)

The immense Spanish Plaza sprawls between the International Trade Mart and the river. Across it are the Poydras and Canal Street wharves, where you board the *President*, the *Creole Queen*, and the *Cotton Blossom*. (The *Natchez* and the *Bayou Jean Lafitte* may be caught at the Toulouse St. Wharf.)

Extending upriver from the Spanish Plaza is the Rouse Company's $55 million **Riverwalk**, a development of shops and restaurants scheduled for completion in late 1986. Almost in its heart is the marbled marvel, the **Hilton Hotel, Riverside and Towers**. With ten restaurants and lounges and a great health club, the Hilton is virtually a city within a city. You'll see the hotel even if you're not staying in it, because you'll come to hear Pete Fountain and to eat at Kabby's. Some of the hotel's 1,600 rooms are equipped for the handicapped. Concierges take care of things in the tower. Moderate. (2 Poydras Street, New Orleans 70140; 504–561–0500 or call locally for the Hilton toll-free number; all major credit cards)

High tea is served daily from 3 P.M. until 5 P.M. in Le Salon, the cushy lobby lounge of the **Windsor Court Hotel**. Scones, chocolate truffles, dainty sandwiches, tea, and sherry are served along with chamber music, for $7.50. Anglophiles will drop whatever they're doing and instantly check into the English country house in the CBD. House of Windsor through and through, the 330-suite soundproof hotel is built around a $1 million collection of artwork. The concierge in morning coat has seen to the needs of Princess Anne and the Lord Mayor of London, among a host of other august personages. Petite and full suites, all quite grand, are available. Fifteen of the suites have facilities for the handicapped, meals are in the grand Grill Room, and the health club has all manner of fitness business. Expensive. (300 Gravier, New Orleans 70140; 504–523–6000 or 800–262–2662; all major credit cards)

The 375-room **International Hotel,** with its imported Italian marble, oriental rugs, and crystal chandeliers, manages an intimate homey ambience. Handicapped persons can be accommodated, and there is a lounge, a café, a restaurant—even a laundromat. In the 100 rooms of the top three floors there are Chippendales and a concierge. Moderate. (300 Canal Street, New Orleans 70140; 504–581–1300, in Los Angeles 800–662–1930, elsewhere 800–535–7783; all major credit cards)

Across the street is **Canal Place**—an enclosed mall with a stunning three-level atrium and entrances on Canal and Iberville streets. It houses pricey places such as Saks, Gucci, and Brooks Brothers. There are about 40 shops in which to spend your money, and many cafés where you can pause to ponder what on earth possessed you to do so. Canal Place details are in *Shopping.*

Glittery glass-enclosed elevators glide up and down over the splashing plaza fountain of Canal Place. You can ascend in one of them to the **Westin Canal Place** on the 11th floor—or you can drop down on its roof in the chopper which delivers VIPs to the hotel from airports in New Orleans and nearby cities. In any case, you'll step into a sunlit rose-colored Carrara marble lobby with period furnishings, fresh flowers, and 26-foot-high windows which frame the river and

the Quarter. You'll enjoy listening to the Original Camellia Jazz Band at luxury Le Jardin's Sunday Brunch.
There is an awesome display of marble, custom-made
millwork and assorted finery in the hotel's 450 peach,
rose, or green rooms. Expensive. (100 Iberville Street,
New Orleans 70130; 504–566–7006 or 800–223–
5672; AE, MC, V)

You can snack, sip cocktails, and hear great jazz
every day from noon until midnight in the **Sheraton
Hotel** lobby. There are five restaurants and lounges in
the 1,200-room hotel. Sixty rooms are reserved for
nonsmokers; four have facilities for the handicapped.
Bathroom phones and other frills are in the eight
floors of the Towers. Moderate. (500 Canal Street,
New Orleans 70130; 504–525–2500 or 800–325–
2525; all major credit cards)

The jazz is matched beat for beat across the street
in the **Marriott,** with the Lobby and Levee lounges
bouncing sounds back and forth day and night. Rooms
are in the 41-story River Tower and the 21-story
Quarter Tower. VIP treatment can be obtained in 28
rooms of the River Tower. All 1,329 rooms and 99
suites have king- or queen-sized beds, or two doubles.
Guests can keep fit in the well-equipped health club.
The Riverview occupies the top spot for supping, see-
ing the sights down below, and enjoying the Sunday
Jazz Brunch. Moderate. (555 Canal Street, New Orleans 70140; 504–581–1000 or 800–228–9290; all
major credit cards)

If it's a Gallic flavor you favor, point your *pieds* to
the **Meridien Hotel.** Air France's $65 million marble
palace is deluxe all the way from the lobby waterfall to
the Tower Suite's 30th-floor duplexes. The high-tech
phone control centers do everything but trim your
toenails; they even broadcast automatic announce-
ments in case catastrophe strikes! Everything you'd
ever need for a long and happy life is enclosed in the

pink marble city. Even if you don't check in, check out the dixieland in the center lobby. Singles, doubles, and suites available. Expensive. (614 Canal Street, New Orleans 70130; 504–525–6500; all major credit cards)

Pete's Pub in the **Hotel Inter-Continental** is a Thirties-style speakeasy, with jazz, an oyster bar, and pub lunches. A marble-and-mirror escalator whisks you to the hotel lobby, where you'll see the collection of original artwork and the sculpture garden in the atrium annex. You can work out at the rooftop health club and gain weight in the gourmet Les Continents restaurant. Expensive. (444 St. Charles, New Orleans 70130; 504–525–5566 or 800–327–0200; all major credit cards)

Nearby, at 545 St. Charles, you'll see the Greek Revival masterpiece, **Gallier Hall,** which was city hall when this was the American Sector. It overlooks the city's second oldest square, named in honor of the Marquis de Lafayette. On Camp Street, across Lafayette Square, is **St. Patrick's Church,** patterned after York Minster in England. One of the architects of the church was an Irishman named James Gallagher, who changed his name to Gallier after moving to New Orleans. It was he who designed Gallier Hall. In the 19th century, Gallier Hall, Lafayette Square, and St. Patrick's were to the Americans what the Cabildo, the Place d'Armes, and St. Louis Cathedral were to the Creoles.

At Poydras and Baronne, the smart monogrammed awnings and graceful *portecochère* (driveway) belong to **Hotel Le Pavillon.** Inside its belle epoque lobby are shimmering imported chandeliers and statuary, and a white marble railing which was once at home in the Grand Hotel of Paris. Le Pavillon's 226 rooms and suites are unusually large, with imported furniture and paintings. Pool and patio are on the roof, cocktail lounge and restaurant in the cellar. Rooms and suites available. Moderate. (Poydras at Baronne, New Orleans 70112; 504–581–3111 or 800–535–9095; all major credit cards)

Legend has it that Huey Long built Airline Highway so as to connect Baton Rouge with the Roosevelt
Hotel. The Roosevelt's been the **Fairmont** since 1965,
and it is everybody's idea of a grand hotel. The live-
ried doormen have ushered in presidents, princes, and
kings. The Sazerac Bar is a favorite watering hole;
when you stop in you'll see why. The legendary Blue
Room has been going strong since 1935. All of the 750
rooms and 50 suites have down pillows, HBO, electric
shoe buffers and sundry frills. The health club and
concierge are both there when you need them. Expensive. (University Place, New Orleans 70140; 504–529–
7111, 800–527–4727, or in Texas, 800–492–6622; all
major credit cards)

Across the street from the Fairmont is the ornate
Beaux Arts **Orpheum Theatre,** within which the New
Orleans Symphony plays and jazz concerts can be
heard. Not far away is the **Saenger Theatre,** where the
likes of Liza Minnelli perform and touring Broadway
shows are mounted.

Across from the Civic Center, the downtown
Howard Johnson's has 300 rooms, many with balconies and facilities for the handicapped, free in-house
movies, parking, and the familiar ice cream parlor restaurant. Inexpensive. (330 Loyola, New Orleans
70112; 504–581–1600 or 800–535–7830; all major
credit cards)

The Poydras Plaza Shopping Mall is dominated
by the enormous **Hyatt Regency Hotel.** The signa-
ture terraced atrium soars 260 feet, glass elevators
prowl up and down its 32 floors, and a wide ramp
connects the hotel with the Superdome. There are five
lively lounges and restaurants, including Top of the
Dome, New Orleans's only revolving restaurant. Standard rooms have king-sized or two double beds, and
the key-access Regency Club on the 27th floor has a
private club and other perks. Handicapped guests can
be accommodated in 12 of the Hyatt's rooms. Moder-

ate. (500 Poydras Street, New Orleans 70140; 504–561–1234 or 800–228–9000; all major credit cards)

The mammoth **Superdome** sprawls out over about 11 acres of what was once a notorious no-man's land known as the Swamp. (Civilized as the Stadium is during the day, it's not recommended that you wander around the area at night.) Home to the NFL's Saints, host to the Sugar Bowl and sometimes the Super Bowl, the Dome is the largest facility of its kind in the world. You can find out all the statistics and see the whole thing on a guided tour. Call 587–3810 for info.

After a $78 million renovation, the old Jung hotel is the new **Clarion.** The 18-story, 759-room hotel has a 24-hour deli, lobby bars, exercise room, and convenient in-house laundromat. Right on the bus route. Inexpensive. (1520 Canal Street, New Orleans 70112; 504–522–4500 or 800–824–3359; all major credit cards)

Among the several motels on the lakeside of Loyola Avenue are: the **Econo Lodge Downtown Motel,** 1725 Tulane Avenue, New Orleans 70112, 504–529–5411 or 800–446–6900. Inexpensive. **Days Inn,** $41–$53, at 1630 Canal Street, New Orleans 70112, 504–586–0110 or 800–325–2525. Inexpensive. Both have pools, coffee shops, parking, accept all major credit cards, and are convenient to the Superdome and the CBD.

Mid-City

By all means visit City Park. And don't worry if you don't have a car to get there. The Esplanade Avenue bus rolls right into the park and stops in front of the **New Orleans Museum of Art.** The Museum's collection is housed in a lovely white neo-classical structure, and includes pre-Colombian art, Italian paintings from the 13th–18th centuries, and an Impressionist Room with a portrait of Evelyn Musson done by her cousin Edgar Degas during a visit here. Admission $3. Open Tuesday–Sunday, 10 A.M. to 5 P.M. (Lelong Avenue, New Orleans 70179; 504–488–2631)

With 1,500 acres, **City Park** is one of the largest, and certainly one of the most magnificent, parks in the country. Once part of the Allard Plantation, the lush park is a terrific place for jogging, picnicking, biking, or just lazing around. Worth the trip in and of themselves are the splendid gnarled old live oaks, draped in frilly shawls of Spanish moss. Legend has it that hot-blooded Creoles faced each other with rapier and pistol beneath the **Duelling Oaks** (near the museum). At the **Casino** on Dreyfous, also near the museum, you can rent a canoe and drift out among the swans on dreamy lagoons. Canoe and bike rentals cost $3.50 an hour. In the park you can also fish, play tennis ($4 an hour), or play golf on your choice of four courses ($8 greens fee). **City Park Stables** (282–6200) at Marconi and Filmore, near the Orleans Avenue border of the park, offer guided trail rides on mild-mannered beasts for $15 an hour. Kids will get a kick out of the Mother Goose characters at **Storyland** and the old carousel at the amusement park. Everybody will enjoy the 15-minute ride on the Gay Nineties miniature train. Call 482–4888 or 486–0799 for all sorts of info.

Garden District & Uptown

Clanging along pretty St. Charles Avenue on the **St. Charles Streetcar** is the best way to take in the Garden District and Uptown sights. (It's also the leisurely way to get to Audubon Zoo—the most direct route is via the Magazine Street bus.) Don't try to do the Garden District and the zoo all in one day.

Along the way to the Garden District you'll pass **Lee Circle,** with its 16-foot statue of General Robert E. Lee atop a 60-foot pedestal. If you're confused by all the "upriver" and "downriver" directions here, this is the place to get your bearings. The General is staring directly north.

Civil War buffs should make a beeline for the **Confederate Museum,** just a block away at 929 Camp Street. Dedicated in 1891, the museum contains all sorts of pertinent memorabilia, including weapons, old maps, part of Lee's camp silver service, and personal effects of Jefferson Davis. Open daily except Sunday, 10 A.M. to 4 P.M. Admission is $2.

If contemporary art is your cup of tea, you'll be right at home in the **Contemporary Arts Center** at 900 Camp. There are changing gallery exhibits and an on-going lineup of plays, dance performances, and jazz, jazz, jazz. Open from noon until 5 P.M. daily except Monday; gallery admission $2.

The **YMCA** at Lee Circle has accommodations for both men and women (the sixth floor is reserved for ladies). Its 200 rooms range from a single at $15 to quads at $42. The Y has a restaurant, pool, and a health club to which shuttle buses bring guests from hotels which have no such luxury. Rooms are spartan but clean. (936 St. Charles Avenue, New Orleans 70130; 504–568–9622; MC, V)

There are several lodging alternatives on or near the streetcar line between Lee Circle and the Garden District. **Quality Inn, Maison St. Charles** is a good buy for those on a budget and it is in a great location. The Inn has a pool, jacuzzi, restaurant, and lounge. Parking is free; the streetcar runs right in front. Inexpensive. (1319 St. Charles Avenue, New Orleans 70130; 504–522–0187 or 800–228–5151; all major credit cards)

For many parents, the very next act after enrolling a child in Tulane is the booking of a room at the **Pontchartrain Hotel** for graduation week. Built in 1927 by the Aschaffenburgs and still lovingly operated by the family, the Pontchartrain is *the* place to stay in the Garden District. Its smart red canopy is a New Orleans landmark, and inside—subdued luxury all the way. There are no pools here, no Nautilus rigs, gift shops, or balconies. There are no computers, either.

But with 225 employees—three for every two guests—the hotel is famous virtually the world over for its personal attention and individualized service. A secluded VIP section? What effrontery! Every guest is a VIP. Just off the hotel's marble vaulted lobby you'll find an endangered species known as the elevator operator—this variety in spotless white gloves. Several of the Pontchartrain's opulent suites are named for the famous for whom the hotel is, or was, home away from home—Mary Martin and the late Richard Burton, for example. No need to pack that grand piano—there's one in the Manhattan Suite. But there are also standard rooms, comfortably furnished, and your bed will be turned down regardless. The posh Caribbean Room is a local favorite, and the Bayou Bar is also popular. Moderate. (2031 St. Charles Avenue, New Orleans 70140; 504–524–0581 or 800–952–8092; all major credit cards)

Have you fond memories of a tête-à-tête at the second floor restaurant of the Eiffel Tower? Well, you'll be able to recapture the moment in the **Restaurant de la Tour Eiffel.** After the Parisian landmark was renovated in 1981, and following a careful search for a city with a suitable ambience to which it could be relocated, the entire restaurant was dismantled and transported from the City of Light to the Crescent City. Its scheduled May 1986 opening is eagerly awaited by New Orleanians and all other romantics. It'll be at 2040 St. Charles Avenue.

That miniature "trolley" you've seen darting around the Quarter with a saxophonist on its aft-deck belongs to the **Avenue Plaza,** in the next block of St. Charles. That stroke of public relations genius is a free shuttle which scoots hotel guests about town. In addition to that attention-getter, the hotel offers 200 rooms and 50 suites, all of which have wet bar, refrigerator, and cable television. A rooftop sundeck, courtyard pool, and luxury health spa with jacuzzi and sauna complete the picture. Inexpensive. (2111 St. Charles Avenue, New Orleans 70130; 504–566–1212 or 800–535–9575; all major credit cards)

First Street and St. Charles is an excellent place to hop off the streetcar and stroll around the Garden District. Many of the district's landmarks are between St. Charles Avenue and First, Camp, and Washington streets. As for the architecture of the grand old homes, it is much like New Orleans food and New Orleans music—an eclectic blend. If you're seriously interested in lintels, dentils, turrets, and dormers, you might pick up a copy of *A Guide to New Orleans Architecture.* The $9 illustrated paperback, published by the local chapter of the American Institute of Architects, is available in most local bookstores. Otherwise, simply enjoy the sights as you would a feast prepared from secret family recipes.

The mansions you'll see are private homes and are not open to the public, except for those which participate in Spring Fiesta tours. One which is open, however, is the **Women's Opera Guild House,** at 2504 Prytania. The interesting, exquisitely furnished house is open Monday–Friday from 1 P.M. until 4 P.M. Admission $2.

If you stroll up Camp Street and turn onto Third you'll see at 1213 the marvelous one-of-a-kind **Montgomery House.** The **Musson House,** 1331 Third, was the home of Michel Musson, a New Orleans postmaster and uncle of Edgar Degas, who often visited the city and this house. Don't miss the **Robinson House** at 1415 Third. One of the largest and loveliest in town, the house is believed to be the first in town to have indoor plumbing. It was built in 1865, right after the Civil War. **Colonel Short's Villa,** at 1448 Fourth, has a cornstalk fence identical to the one at 915 Royal in the Quarter. Not to be sneezed at is the house itself, which was the creation of Henry Howard, the estimable architect of Nottoway Plantation. The delicate confection called the **Grima House,** 1604 Fourth, at the corner of St. Charles, was concocted in about 1850.

Affiliated with American Youth Hostels, the **Marquette House** is an 80-bed dormitory-style hostelry just one block off the streetcar line on Carondelet Street. Private rooms are occasionally available, and there is a kitchen, a lounge, and a garden patio. Hostel members pay $8 per night, nonmembers $9.75. You can speak with someone in the office between 7 A.M. and 10 A.M., and between 5 P.M. and 11 P.M.; at other times an answering machine will take your message. Marquette House accepts no credit cards, but if you have proper identification they will take traveler's checks. (2253 Carondelet Street, New Orleans 70130; 504–523–3014)

The Crescent City Skating Rink was built in about 1885 at the corner of Washington and Prytania. The old building now houses **The Rink,** a shopping mall chock full of terrific places to shop and indulge yourself. **Indulgence** is a many-windowed restaurant with pretty floral-print wallpaper. Sweetbreads, chicken, quail, and veal are all prepared with the freshest of fresh ingredients here. For dessert, you'll be well satisfied with either fruit tarts or white chocolate mousse pie. About $50 for two. (2727 Prytania; 504–899–4411; AE, MC, V)

If you've not found what you're looking for at the Rink, the marvels of Magazine Street are not far away. Since you're on your way to Audubon Park, why not stop at **Magazine Cuisine,** 3242 Magazine, 504–899–9453, and pick up a picnic of deli sandwiches, cheese, and wine? It's open Monday–Saturday, 10:30 A.M. to 7:30 P.M., and Sundays, 11 A.M. to 4 P.M. If picnicking is not your style, Flagons, A Wine Bar, is nearby (discussed in *Dining*), and its neighbor is **Monroe's.** You can put together a fine bunch of garden things at the salad bar for $8, or you can get down to serious business with barbecued ribs, steaks, prime ribs, and seafood. Entrées are from $8 to $18. (3218 Magazine; 504–891–1897; AE, MC, V)

Bayou Blue is a very casual family-style spot over on Prytania. The menu is po-boys, jambalaya, and red beans and rice, and the ambience is down-home. It's open for breakfast, lunch, and dinner, and the prices are quite modest. Dinner for two will be around $20. (3625 Prytania; 504–897–6100; MC, V)

The Garden District lies on part of the old Livaudais Plantation, which later was incorporated as the city of Lafayette and still later, in 1852, annexed by the growing city of New Orleans. Bounded by Washington, Coliseum, Prytania, and Sixth streets, **Lafayette Cemetery #1** was the burial grounds of the city of Lafayette. Among its old vaults and tombs is the monument of the Jefferson Fire Company #22, with a marble bas-relief depicting an old 1830s engine and pumper. Many victims of the 1850s flue epidemics are buried in this old cemetery, which was established in 1833.

Commander's Palace, at 1403 Washington (detailed in *Dining*), is tops on your must-do list. The picturesque turreted old house has been a restaurant since 1883 and was the birthplace of the jazz brunches which are now Sunday staples all over town.

If you happen to be in the 3600 block of St. Charles on a Wednesday evening and come across what appears to be a block party, it's the weekly "three drinks for the price of one" night at **Que Sera,** an extremely popular Garden District eating and drinking establishment. The Wednesday night do is a great draw. Portable bars are set up outside to take care of the doctors, lawyers, secretaries, executives, students, and professors from Loyola and Tulane who turn out in droves for the drinks. Que Sera is a great gathering place *every* day (it's open daily from 11 A.M. until 11 P.M., later on weekends) and a fine spot to stop off for a drink. Preferred seating is on the porch overlooking the joggers, the streetcar, and the avenue's trees. (3636 St. Charles Avenue, New Orleans 70115; 504–897–2598; AE, DC, MC, V)

Adjoining Que Sera are the tiny lobby and two floors of the **St. Charles Inn**—a very good buy. It's not a luxurious place, but rooms are large, well-lit, and carpeted. All have color television, air-conditioning, and separate dressing area with vanity. A newspaper is delivered daily to your door. Continental breakfast included in the room rate. A parking lot adjoins it. Inexpensive. (3636 St. Charles Avenue, New Orleans 70115; 504–899–8888; all major credit cards)

The **Columns Hotel** has been featured in so many films it probably should be a member of the Screen Actors Guild. Interior shots for Brooke Shields's *Pretty Baby* and scenes for Clint Eastwood's *Tightrope* and for the recent *Down by Law* were all filmed in this picturesque old house. Locals love its Victorian lounge, with its well-worn sofas, red leather upholstered booths, and white lace curtains. The ambience here is of an old country home. The "patio" is a wide front porch. Guest rooms are vast seas of sunshine, and big bathrooms have old-fashioned fixtures. There are no phones in the rooms, and if you require a television you'll have to ask for one; they're sometimes available. Only six of the 16 rooms have private baths. There is no pool; meals are served in a fine old dining room. Inexpensive. (3811 St. Charles Avenue, New Orleans; 70115; 504–899–9308; AE, MC, V)

Audubon Park & Audubon Zoo

Once the Foucher Plantation where, in 1795, Etienne de Bore discovered the process by which sugar could be granulated, **Audubon Park** is a luxuriant 400-acre uptown utopia for joggers, bikers, fisher-folk, roller skaters, and loafers. In 1884–85, it was the site for New Orleans's first World's Fair, and the 18-hole golf course near the St. Charles Avenue entrance is in the area once covered by what was at one time the largest building in the world—an architectural ancestor of the Superdome.

Frederick Law Olmsted, designer of New York's Central Park, had a hand in landscaping Audubon Park. With all due respect to Gotham, New York's version lacks the natural profusion of palms, majestic live oaks, magnolias, and thick green carpeting which makes Audubon Park the tropical paradise that it is. A statue of naturalist John J. Audubon, shaded in a grove of trees, gazes out over the urban oasis which bears his name. He appears well pleased.

If golf is your game, head for the clubhouse at Walnut and Hurst near the uptown border of the park. The greens fee is $6 weekdays, $9 weekends, and you can rent a set of clubs for $6. Clubhouse phone—864-8260. Just to the right of the St. Charles entrance to the park is the first of 18 exercise stations on a one-and-a-half-mile jogging track. The track runs through an alley of live oaks and is shaded by a leafy green arch. Parallel to St. Charles, Magazine Street splits the park in half, and at the park's mid-section (roughly speaking), Natatorium Walk leads off Magazine to the tennis courts ($4 an hour) and to Audubon Park Stables (guided trail rides at $20 an hour—phone 897-2817). Not far away is the **Mombasa Safari mini-tram,** which departs every half hour for a tour through the grasslands of the zoo. It'll cost you a buck to board it, and you'll love it.

Audubon Zoo comprises 58 acres of the park on the riverside, about ¾ of a mile from St. Charles Avenue. If you arrive on the Magazine Street bus, you'll get off just across from the zoo. From St. Charles Avenue, you can either stroll alongside the golf course in the direction of the river, or you can take the free shuttle bus through the park. The shuttle picks up passengers every 15 or 20 minutes in front of Tulane University and delivers them to the zoo. Zoo admission is $4.50 for adults, $2 for senior citizens and children 2–12, and strollers can be rented for $2.

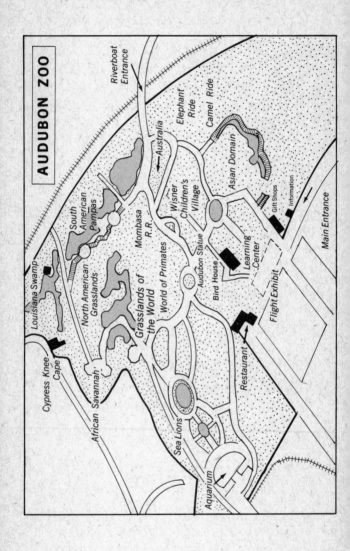

AUDUBON ZOO

Riverboat Entrance

South American Pampas

Australia

Elephant Ride

Camel Ride

Mombasa R.R.

Wisner Children's Village

Asian Domain

Gift Shops

Information

Louisiana Swamp

North American Grasslands

Grasslands of the World

World of Primates

Audubon Statue

Bird House

Learning Center

Main Entrance

Cypress Knee Cape

African Savannah

Sea Lions

Restaurant

Flight Exhibit

Aquarium

There is a Zootique where you can buy Zoovenirs, and the zoo is open every day from 9:30 A.M. until 5 P.M.

It is a wonderful zoo. One hundred years old in 1985, Audubon Zoo is now considered one of the top five zoos in the country. More than 1,000 animals roam in naturalistic habitats beautifully landscaped with waterfalls, caves, lakes, rocky ridges and grasslands. A wooden walkway loops through the various sections, where animals indigenous to a particular region all share the land and the water. In the Australian Exhibit, kangaroos hop past wallabies and snooty emu; a giraffe in the African Savannah nibbles the leaves of a tree, watched by a nearby gazelle. There's the Asian Domain, South American Pampas, North American Grasslands, World of Primates, a reptile house, bird sanctuary, and the petting zoo. Not far from the levee you'll see Monkey Hill. Locals say it was designed to show children in these flatlands what a hill looks like. Down on the levee is the landing for the *Cotton Blossom.* A relaxing downriver cruise on the paddlewheeler is a fine way to wind up a day at the former Foucher Plantation.

Wrapped in verandahs, draped in flags, the pretty pink-and-white **Park View Guest House,** on the National Register of Historic Places, was built in 1884 to accommodate visitors in town for the Cotton Exposition. Ring the bell by the lovely leaded glass door, and step into an airy lobby where black-and-white tile floors are polished to a high shine and hanging baskets overflow with greenery. In the dining room, the original Waterford crystal chandelier shines over tables covered with white linen, where you have your hot croissants, orange juice, and coffee (complimentary); large windows let you look out upon the green serenity of Audubon Park. Massive carved armoires and canopied beds are almost dwarfed in the guesthouse's 25 spacious rooms, and sunlight splashes through full-length windows. The sole TV set is in the first floor public room, and phone calls are made from pay phones on each floor. Accommodations available with both private and semi-private bath. Inexpensive. (7004 St. Charles Avenue, New Orleans 70118; 504–861–7564; MC, V)

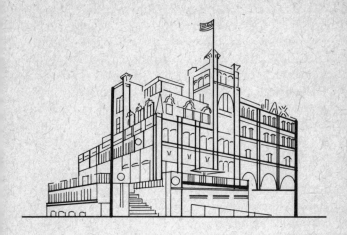

Shopping

New Orleans is one of the greatest shopping cities in the country. Its chic antique stores are justly famous, as are the musty, serendipitous bazaars where bargaining is a favorite pastime.

French Quarter streets are lined with fascinating shops. In the 100–900 blocks of Royal Street you can find everything from priceless antiques to pralines. Exquisite 18th century furniture, decorative accessories, jewelry, and silver can be found at **Dixon & Dixon** (#237), **Rothschild's** (#241 and #321), **Royal Antiques** (#307), **Waldhorn** (#343), **Manheim** (#403), and **M.S. Rau** (#610). **Henry Stern** (#329) specializes in 17th and 18th century French and English antiques, and the **French Antique Shop** (#225) features French chandeliers and furnishings. Rare coins and antique weapons are bought, sold, and "horse traded" at **James H. Cohen & Sons** (#437). If you've been hankering for a carousel horse, you'll find some beauties along with brass decorative accessories at **The Brass Lion** (#516). Contemporary graphics are showcased at **Nahan Galleries** (#540) and **Hanson Galleries** (#229). **Bryant Galleries** (#524) has Haitian, European, and American sculpture and graphics, and there is a stunning Erte collection among the treasures at **Dyansen Gallery** (#433). Renoirs, Turners, and Corots are at the **Fine Arts Gallery** (#313). **Rumors** (#513), an upscale gift and jewelry shop, has fantastic masks made by Andrew Leit. Tucked into a courtyard at #623 is the **Loom Room,** with American crafts and woolens. Stop in **Kate Latter's** (#300) for pralines, gifts, and jellies. At the 100-year-old **Bourbon French Perfume Co.** (#318), you can buy a ready-made fragrance or have one custom-made just for you. The nostalgic clothing and frilly millinery at **Fleur de Paris** (#712) is to swoon over, but if you're of a more modern bent, bop into **Bongo's** (#918) for New Wave styles.

But Royal is only one of the Quarter's fascinating streets. Chartres Street has its charms, among them **Ye Olde Pipe Shoppe,** at #306, where you can see an antique pipe collection, have your pipe repaired, or buy a new one. On Conti Street, you can find that whale vertebrae you've been looking for. It's at **Endangered Species,** #604, along with Hindu temple carvings, mounted tusks, and other exotic things from Africa, Asia, and the Middle East. At the **Quarter Smith,** 509 Conti, you can have your fine jewelry repaired, create your own jewelry design, or buy contemporary, antique, and estate gems. Don't miss the **Coghlan Gallery,** 710 Toulouse Street. Its peaceful courtyard is filled with fountains and statuary and garden accessories, all crafted by local artists. In Cabildo Alley, the **Cabildo Emporium** makes Panama hats and imports sweaters, ponchos, and rugs from South America. On Dumaine Street, all sorts of patchwork things are at the **Old Craft Cottage** (#511), and all sorts of everything can be found at the **Useful Shop** (#519)—zany hardware, motor oil, "flip-flop" sandals, sunglasses, umbrellas, etc. Nostalgics will go nuts over the old coin-operated machines and jukeboxes at the **Dumaine Nostalgia Shop** (#607). **The Witch-**

craft Shop, at 521 St. Philip, is your one-stop shop for how-to-voodoo and gris-gris.

Yet more hours can be spent prowling the shops along Decatur Street. The **Jax Brewery** is a splashy shopping complex where clowns, jazz bands, and balloons often add zest to the already zippy scene. Wide open spaces and strategically placed escalators let you see what's in stores for you as you ride up and down. Sweet scents of soaps and sachets let you know **Crabtree & Evelyn** is nearby. **Hats in the Belfry** has Panama hats, sophisticated chapeaux, and silly caps. **Giggles** has a laughing stock of silk-screen designs on tote bags and T-shirts. Elegant and eccentric accessories are at **the Kendall Kollection;** natural fiber and hand-crocheted clothing can be found at **Alexia's.** At the **New Orleans School of Cooking**'s retail shop you can buy Creole and Cajun cookbooks, as well as the ingredients you'll need for the recipes, and if you planned ahead you can take a cooking lesson. **La Belle Epoque** will sell you one of its "Perfume of New Orleans" fragrances. The **Jubilee Market** is a colorful cavalcade of pushcarts filled with collectibles, and at the third floor **JAXFEST** you can eat barbecued ribs, burgers and fries, fried chicken, red beans and rice. Tables are inside and out, and the terrace is a fine place for munching, imbibing, and watching Old Man River roll along.

Noted local artist Lois Rebstock paints Louisiana plantation homes on delicate glass Christmas ornaments, and you can buy them at **Plantation Country,** across from the Brewery at 615 Decatur. Her shop also is a bonanza for *Gone With the Wind* fiends. Downriver apiece, candymakers, cafés, ice-cream stands, and colorful shops are laced in amid the colonnades and arcades of the **French Market.** At **Aunt Sally's Praline Shop** you can watch the candy being made before you buy it. You'll find records, decorations, and New Orleans memorabilia at **All That Jazz,** and handmade bisque dolls and Cajun storybooks at **The Little Toy Shop.** Thimbles, charms, pottery, and pewter are at **Bijouterie;** flowers, baskets, handmade masks, hammocks, and hats are sold at the **Bazaar.** Go to **Manila Galleon** for beaded and embroidered blouses, porcelain, woks, and inlaid wood, and to **Four Seasons Emporium** for natural fiber clothing and accessories. On weekends, the flea market behind the Farmer's Market sprawls out into the street, and **Reality Market** is but one of several indoor flea markets in that area. The **Marketplace,** at 1015 Decatur, is an indoor mall of fascinating shops selling everything from mosquito nets and hammocks to handmade masks and handcrafted jewelry.

Canal Place is a ritzy enclosed mall of many-splendored things in the 300 block of Canal Street, linking Canal with Iberville Street in the Quarter. **Saks** escalates all the way from plaza to terrace to stunning atrium level, and about 40 other retail shops surround the bubbling plaza fountain. Men's and women's wear is at **Benetton, Brooks Brothers, Polo/Ralph Lauren,** and **Gokeys'.** Ladies can also be outfitted at **Guy Laroche, Christian Aujard, Laura Ashley, Cactus,** and **Cache,** and find shoes at **Charles Jourdan** and **Bergeron's.** Both men and women can be shod at **Bally's of Switzerland** or **Gucci.** New Orleans designer **Mignon Paget** creates men's and women's jewelry of sterling, 14K gold, and bronze d'ore. You can buy a book and read it too at **Upstart Crow's** combination bookstore/restaurant. There are cuddly things at **Classy Bears** and joyous toys at **FAO Schwarz.** Among Canal Place's eateries are the **Panda Café** and the **American Backyard Grill.**

If you take the Magazine Street bus at Canal and Magazine, in about ten minutes you'll be in a browser's heaven. Most of Magazine's six miles of shops are in gingerbread Victorian houses and quaint little cottages. Six miles is a bit much to detail. But a few of the many noteworthy places to look for are the **Poke Around Place** (#2907), where the weak-willed can poke around forever in the old furniture, bric-a-brac, and goodness knows what; **A Collector's Book Shop** (#3119), with its old and rare books; and **Second Hand Rose** (#3110), which has 100 years of antique clothing from 1850 to 1950. **Ages Ago** (#3113) has depression glass, kitchenware, fine linens, all from . . . ages ago. Merry-go-round horses, old coin-operated machines, and vintage clothing, costumes, and dolls are at **Carousel Antiques** (#3944). China, brass, copper, and decoys are at **Queen Flea** (#3955), and all of your needlework needs are at the **Persian Cat** (#5513). Men's discount clothes are at **Claude's** (#5523), and women's discount shoes are at the **Shoe Outlet** (#5419). If you want to add to your inactive silverware pattern, try **As You Like It** (#3929).

The St. Charles Streetcar will take you to the **Uptown Square** and **Riverbend** shopping centers. To reach the former, get off at Broadway and walk six blocks toward the river, where you'll find more than 70 shops housed in medieval-style buildings. You'll find Riverbend right where the streetcar turns on South Carrollton. Dante Street and Hampson Street are lined with turn-of-the-century Creole cottages, now filled with bustling boutiques.

And all of that is but the merest hint of the treasures to be unearthed in the Crescent City.

Dining

Some folks have literally waxed lyrical about South Louisiana food. This is the happy home of "jambalaya, crawfish pie, and filé gumbo." Creole and Cajun cooking is America's only distinctive regional cuisine. The former is New Orleans's rich "city slicker" version, while the latter—found in abundance in the area described in the last section of this book—is the culinary equivalent of its earthy country cousin. Don't try to figure out differences between them. There are many cross-over dishes, and most chefs nowadays say that over the years the two traditions have merged into "South Louisiana-style cooking." Food down here is different, delicious, and rich, rich, rich—a gourmet's dream come true and a dieter's nightmare.

This region has an embarrassment of seafood riches and an abundance of heady herbs and spices. Shrimp and crawfish (tiny "toy lobster"-like critters) show up in a wide variety of dishes, including a thick tomato-based sauce called *étouffée* (ay-too-fay), and you won't have to look far for an oyster bar. New Orleanians consume tons of oysters—raw, fried, boiled, and

Rockefeller. Barbecued shrimp, very popular here, is not barbecued at all but cooked in a butter-and-garlic sauce and placed before you whole, with head, legs, and tails intact. You roll up your sleeves, ask for more napkins, and go at them with your fingers. Local chefs do magical things with a simple staple such as rice. Jambalaya is made with rice, spices, and seafood, chicken, or sausage; red beans and rice, traditionally served on Mondays in New Orleans, consists of kidney beans cooked down to a thick creamy sauce, mixed with rice, and often flavored with chunks of a spicy hot sausage called andouille (roughly, *ahń-doo-wee*). Rice is always an ingredient in gumbo, a thick soup which may also contain okra, seafood, chicken, or andouille. (Filé, pronounced *fée-lay*, is ground sassafras leaves and is used for seasoning.) A favorite Creole breakfast is grillades (*gree-yahds*) and grits, the former being squares of veal simmered in stock. *Pain perdu,* or lost bread, is akin to French toast and so-called because the day-old French bread with which it's made is used rather than tossed out, or "lost." You'll meet the muffuletta here, and the po-boy; both are sandwich marvels. A muffuletta is ham, Italian sausages, cheeses, and olive salad between huge rounds of seeded bread. You can buy either half or a whole, and you'd better be hungry if you get it whole. The po-boy—originally a nickel lunch for—yep, poor boys—is similar to the submarine or hero, only much more intense. (Incidentally, a "dressed" sandwich here comes with "the works.")

Desserts in these parts are especially extravagant. Bananas Foster is cinnamon-spiced bananas sautéed in butter and liqueurs, flamed with brandy and served over ice cream. The ubiquitous bread pudding can be either a cake-like square swimming in whiskey sauce or thick cinnamony custard topped with frothy meringue. It's different every place it's served and, despite its plain-Jane name, is definitely not to be sneezed at. A praline parfait is a soft version of the popular patty and is sometimes, but not always, flavored with a praline liqueur. Beignets (*ben-yéas*) are square-shaped, hole-less doughnuts liberally dusted with powdered sugar. (Try not to inhale as you aim one of these at your open mouth—you'll have a coughing fit.) And New Orleanians drink gallons of powerful coffee laced with chicory (a ground herb) and often served *au lait.*

There are many other exotic regional dishes, and local waiters are accustomed to explaining them to the city's visitors.

If you pay your restaurant bill by credit card, you'll see that only the total amount appears on the slip you sign—the tax line is left blank. That's *your* "tip" that local waiters expect a gratuity based on the total bill, not just the amount before taxes. Tip here as you would any place else—about 15 percent, and according to the service you receive.

Again, credit card abbreviations are: AE, American Express; CB, Carte Blanche; DC, Diners Club; MC, MasterCard; V, Visa. "All major credit cards" means that all of these cards will be accepted.

Except as otherwise noted prices quoted are for two, not including wine, drinks, or tip.

It's a good idea to call first and check a restaurant's current credit card policies, dress code, etc. These things do have a way of changing.

Breakfast

In antebellum New Orleans, Creole breakfasts were long and leisurely, with several courses stretched out over three hours or more. At **Brennan's,** you can capture the spirit of those days, and while $20 apiece may seem steep for breakfast, this is not your ordinary ham and eggs. There are rich Creole soups and baked apples with double cream. Egg dishes—Benedict, Hussarde, Sardou, and so on, are each topped with perhaps the best Hollandaise sauce in the world. You'll have slowed down considerably by the time the Bananas Foster arrives, and you may have to go home and lie down after so much richness. If you can't handle all of that, there are omelets in the $10 to $12 range (the Eggs Portuguese in flaky pastry shells are divine) and luncheon specials at about the same price. This beautiful building dates from 1795, and once housed the Banque de la Louisiane. Due to its fame—and popularity with the locals—you'll probably have to nurse a drink in the pretty patio while waiting for your table, even if you have made a reservation (essential!). The brunch crowd often comes casual, but dinner is strictly dress-up—and more expensive. Open seven days. (417 Royal Street; 504–525–9711; AE, MC, V)

The Coffee Pot is an easygoing café next door to Pat O'Brien's. Office workers gather here regularly during the week for coffee, and on Sundays you'll see Quarter locals reading the morning paper and working crosswords. Don't come here if you're in a hurry! Service is notoriously slow, but the carriageway is a fine place to linger over a plantation breakfast of ham, eggs, grits, and Pearl's plump hot biscuits (which come with lots of butter and jelly). There's a full varied menu as well, the bread pudding is legendary, and the warm pecan pie topped with whipped cream is the best in town. Breakfast is served all day, into the night, at anywhere from $5 to $15. (714 St. Peter; 504–524–3500; AE, MC, V)

A body can get a hearty breakfast at **Tranchina's** for about two bucks, and that amazingly low price includes the bacon and the biscuits! Located in the CBD, this restaurant has been serving good solid food at reasonable prices since the 1890s, and that tradition continues under its new management. There's a daily blue-plate special, steaks, salads, and a long list of sandwiches. Friendly and casual, every day of the week. (729 Common Street; 504–524–5358; AE, MC, V)

Open 24 Hours

It's a New Orleans tradition to end a night of revelry at **Café du Monde** on Jackson Square. This is the place for those sugary beignets and *café au lait*. (The entire menu, on napkin holders, consists of beignets—three to an order—coffee, milk, and perhaps orange juice.) Each order is 65 cents in this bustling, noisy, and very popular spot. There are a few tables sprinkled around a fountain and a few more inside, but most of them are crammed together on an open-air pavilion. There's a very international flavor in New Orleans's answer to *Café de la Paix* in Paris. Everyone comes here, and it never closes. There's now a second location in the Esplanade Shopping Center. (815 Decatur Street at Jackson Square; 504–561–9235; no credit cards)

    Bailey's, in the Fairmont Hotel, has Tiffany shades, brass rails, stained glass over the bar, and bagels and lox. Breakfast is served around the clock. Selections include eggs Benedict ($6), waffles with lots of whipped butter and blueberry syrup ($4), and danish, omelettes, and cereal in the $2 to $3 range. A big bowl of red beans and rice is $5, the seafood platter is $11.50, and there are burgers, deli sandwiches, and salads. Dinners are from $10 to $12 in this rather classy but casual all-night eatery. (The Fairmont Hotel, 123 Baronne; 504–529–7111; all major credit cards)

French Creole

The 145-year-old **Antoine's** has a bit of a split personality. The good news about America's oldest restaurant is its food, and that, oddly, leads to its negative side. Tourists often leave here with a bad taste in their mouths—not from the food, but from the service they

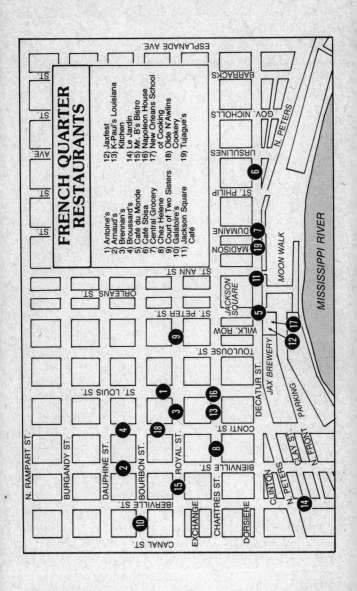

FRENCH QUARTER RESTAURANTS

1) Antoine's
2) Arnaud's
3) Brennan's
4) Broussard's
5) Café du Monde
6) Café Sbisa
7) Central Grocery
8) Chez Helene
9) Court of Two Sisters
10) Galatoire's
11) Jackson Square Café
12) Jaxfest
13) K-Paul's Louisiana Kitchen
14) Le Jardin
15) Mr. B's Bistro
16) Napoleon House
17) New Orleans School of Cooking
18) Olde N'Awlins Cookery
19) Tujague's

receive. Because of its justly famous cuisine and old-world ambience, Antoine's is a great favorite of old-line New Orleanians, who dine here frequently. They reserve a table with their regular waiters, are treated royally, and regard the restaurant as a very exclusive private club. (The usually sedate "grand dame" gives way to nuttiness when a Carnival krewe takes over the premises for an all-night frolic.) Observing the camaraderie between the staff and other customers—usually longtime clients—the tourist may feel like a kid with his nose pressed against a candy store window. Almost anyone will tell you that it's best to go to Antoine's first with a "regular"—and that's true. With its à la carte, all-in-French menu and sometimes aloof service, it can be off-putting. And yet, the restaurant has a souvenir menu, and hands out a souvenir pamphlet packed with trivia about itself, so it certainly recognizes the fact that tourists dine here.

Ah, but the food—there's the good news. Among the house specialties are those world-famous dishes which originated here—oysters Rockefeller, *pompano en papilotte,* and light, incredibly delicious "puffed" potatoes, eaten with your fingers and served in an intricately woven basket of bread and potatoes. Trout almondine is also quite good, and the *filet mignon marchand de vin* is arguably the best in the world. Its best known dessert is Baked Alaska (which you must order at the beginning of your meal), but chocolate mousse is heavenly and the house lights dim for the showy crepes Suzettes and cherries jubilee. After a potent cup of coffee and a tab of about $75, waddle around and savor the charm of this enormous eatery. Note especially the 26,000-bottle wine cellar. Reservations and jackets are essential. (713 St. Louis Street; 504–581–4422; all major credit cards)

Those long lines of well-dressed people on Bourbon Street just before noon and in the evening are waiting to get into **Galatoire's.** The restaurant takes neither reservations nor credit cards and is another of the classic French Creole places favored by well-heeled locals. It's a rather small mirrored room, with lots of polished brass and old-fashioned ceiling fans, in which the champagne set has been consuming seafood, chicken, and steak since around the turn of the century. Oysters are superb—*en brochette* or Rockefeller—as is *crawfish étoufée*, pompano, and trout. Galatoire's is open from 11:30 A.M. until 9 P.M., so you could avoid the lines by arriving very early or around two-ish in the afternoon. Jackets and ties are required after five and all day Sunday (it's closed Mondays), but you'll feel more comfortable a bit gussied up whatever time you arrive. $50 to $60. (209 Bourbon Street; 504–525–2021; no credit cards)

There is something very gentle about **Arnaud's,** another of the old-line restaurants. It's a lovely place with mosaic tile floors, crisp napery, and fresh flowers on discreetly placed tables. Have a before-dinner drink, listen to piano music in the Grill or the elegant Richelieu Bar, and then adjourn to turtle soup or oysters stewed in cream. Follow that with quail, Cornish hen, or trout meuniere; finish up with *crème brulee* or strawberries in cream. The jazz brunch on Sundays is great fun and is a bit less formal than dinner, which is a dress-up affair. Speaking of dresses, a small Mardi Gras exhibit on the second floor displays Carnival gowns worn by Germaine Wells, daughter of "Count" (the title was honorary) Arnaud Cazenave, who founded the restaurant in 1918. A great place. About $60. (813 Bienville; 504–523–5433; all major credit cards)

\/ **Commander's Palace,** operated by the Brennan family, is in every way a splendid experience and should be very high on your list of dining priorities. The rambling old Garden District house is fascinating, with bright sunshiny colors, lovely woodwork, and tropical plants around the patio fountain. (You go through the kitchen to get to the patio.) If you reserve well in advance, you may get into the Garden Room, which has one floor-to-ceiling window overlooking those trees and plants. Commander's jazz brunch may be the best in a city of great jazz brunchers. There are balloons, a peripatetic trio, and a festive ambience. Eggs and things are around $15 at brunch. In the evening, complete dinners of fish, quail, rabbit, or chicken are about $26. Commander's dessert legend is the Celebration—raspberries, liqueurs, ice cream, chocolate, and cream topped with raspberry brandy sauce and flamed at your table. By all means deck yourself out and duck into Commander's Palace. (1403 Washington; 504–899–8221; all major credit cards)

The new kid on the block is **George IV,** a rather chic spot about which word is spreading fast. It's a Rhode family enterprise, and the young chef—he's the fourth George Rhode—worked with the estimable Paul Prudhomme. Here he's added his own touch to some old New Orleans favorites. Crawfish Breaux Bridge is "Cajun popcorn"—peeled crawfish tails, battered, fried, and served with creole mustard sauce. Things like trout in roasted pecan-butter mixture and Long Island Duckling cooked with spicy brandy-laced peach sauce make the decision-making difficult. For dessert, give up and get the Choco-holic. Despite its shopping center location, George IV is rather formal and you'll pay at least $45. (701 Metairie Road; 504–832–3933; all major credit cards)

The pink, plush, and posh **Caribbean Room** is in the luxury Pontchartrain Hotel. It is very theatrical, reflecting the flair of the hotel's owner and attracting celebrities who pay dearly for Trout Eugene and Trout Veronique. (2031 St. Charles Avenue; 504–524–0581; all major credit cards)

In 1856 one Madame Begue served hearty "second breakfasts" to butchers and vendors from the nearby French Market. **Tujague's** (pronounced *two jacks*), the second restaurant on Madame Begue's Decatur Street site, is New Orleans's second oldest eatery. Until very recently you literally took pot luck at Tujague's, since there was only one entrée served daily. The selection is still somewhat limited, but you can usually count on its famous brisket of beef in Creole sauce. It's open daily for lunch ($6 to $12), and the six-course dinners at night are $17 to $20 each. You're sure to conjure up images from the city's flamboyant past in this ancient "very New Orleans" institution. (823 Decatur; 504–525–8676; all major credit cards)

Reservations are absolutely essential at **Corinne Dunbar's.** You'll take cocktails in the drawing room of this gracious antebellum home in the Garden District and then repair to the dining room for a seven-course fixed-price ($22) repast. The tables are a bit too small and a tad too close together, but there is nevertheless the definite sense of dining in the private home of a friend—who naturally wouldn't dream of taking your credit card. Open for dinner only Tuesday through Saturday, 6 P.M. until 10:30 P.M. (1617 St. Charles; 504–525–2957 or 525–0689; no credit cards)

You'll also need to reserve and dress for the occasion when you sup at **Broussard's.** Broussard's is so romantic your knees might get weak when you first step inside. The lighting in the large Napoleon Room is wickedly seductive, and the smaller, somewhat secluded Josephine Room overlooks the very pretty patio. Broussard's has been serving splendid French Creole food for more than 65 years. Pay close attention when your waiter recites the daily specials, and take his advice about what to order. If you order a flaming dessert, don't expect a big show; you don't get to see the fiery works. $55 to $60. (819 Conti Street; 504–581–3866; all major credit cards)

In general, locals are not fond of the **Court of Two Sisters,** but tourists usually love it. One of the Quarter's largest courtyards is loaded with lush greenery, cockatoos and macaws hang around here and there, and a roving jazz band plays daily from 9 A.M. until 3 P.M. during the $15 per person brunch buffet. (613 Royal; 504–522–7261; all major credit cards)

The Gumbo Shop is an informal place where the food is good and the price is certainly right. In addition to its title offering, the restaurant has a combination plate with generous heaps of red beans and rice, shrimp Creole, and jambalaya. A casual, easy restaurant, and two can get out for $20. (630 St. Peter; 504–525–1486; AE, CB, MC, V)

Cajun

New Orleans's resident celebrity chef Paul Prudhomme (who was once the culinary ruler at Commander's Palace) catapulted his **K-Paul's Louisiana Kitchen** into national prominence. His prices have also skyrocketed since the restaurant's modest beginnings in 1979. No doubt about it, this is *the* place to go for blackened redfish and robust Cajun things, but people often complain about the long lines, high prices, and table-sharing policy. K-Paul's takes neither reservations nor plastic, entrées are about $18, and the European custom of sharing a table with strangers has never crossed the Atlantic and caught on here. It's open for dinner only Monday through Friday, and closed on weekends. (416 Chartres; 504–942–7500; no credit cards)

The **Bon Ton Café** has been a hot ticket for two generations. It's chock full of CBD businesspeople at lunchtime, and there's no point in going for dinner at night unless you've reserved a table. The étouffées, jambalaya, redfish, and other Cajun dishes are made from family recipes which go back to Bayou Lafourche. Closed Saturday and Sunday. $35 to $40. (401 Magazine; 504–524–3386; AE, MC, V)

A Lot of Soul . . .

For years and years, **Buster Holmes** Burgundy Street café was *the* place to go for red beans and rice, barbecued ribs, fried chicken, black-eyed peas, greens, and cornbread. It's a hardcore country kitchen that features good food . . . period. Daily plate lunch specials are scrawled outside on a board and cost about $6. There are other locations now—one in the Jax Brewery—and things are not quite the same. But it is still pretty soulful. (921 Burgundy Street; 504–561–9375; no credit cards)

Good-natured Leah Chase presides over the kitchen at **Dooky Chase.** The restaurant has been serving up soul and Creole since 1941, and it is a great local favorite. Only 10 minutes or so from the Saenger or Theatre of Performing Arts, Dooky Chase is open from just before noon until 1 or 2 A.M., seven days a week. You don't really need a reservation, and you'll pay $20 to $25 for two. (2301 Orleans Avenue; 504–822–9506; AE, MC, V)

The soul at **Chez Helene** also draws lots of locals, and the place is so successful that a second restaurant has been opened inside the Hotel de la Poste. There are oysters Rockefeller and Bienville as well as fried chicken and red beans and rice. Open seven days a week, 11 A.M. until 11 P.M. (closes at 7 P.M. on Mondays). $25 to $30. (1540 North Robertson; 504–947–9155; all major credit cards)

French

Things are quite formally French in the Hotel Meridien's **Henri.** Located near the registration desk, the restaurant has two dining levels and is rather serene with its shades of green, polished brass, glass, and marble. The à la carte selections are extensive, quite interesting, and a bit exotic. You'll dine with a dressed-up crowd, but only if you make a reservation. $65 to $70; closed Sundays. (Hotel Meridien, 614 Canal Street; 504–525–6500; all major credit cards)

The *tres intime* **Savoir Faire** is tucked away behind the lobby of the St. Louis Hotel. If you've been casting about for a good place in which to fall in love, this might be just what you're looking for. This small mirrored room fairly winks with romance. And there are *escargots campagnards,* a fine garlic soup, *poulet basquaise, cotes d'agneau Marie Louise, filet de boeuf sauce Madere,* and any number of Gallic dishes which will add up to around $35 to $40. Open 11 A.M. until 11 P.M. Monday through Friday, and for dinner only Saturday and Sunday. (730 Bienville; 504–522–3966; AE, MC, V)

A Wine Bar

Flagons, A Wine Bar (New Orleans's only wine bar, so far), is relatively new and was an almost instant hit with the yuppies. Its wine list is impressive; you can buy wine by the bottle or the glass. You can snack on cheeses or take seriously the à la carte seafoods and pasta. In the latter instance your very pleasant evening will cost $30 to $35. Open for lunch and dinner every day. (3222 Magazine Street; 504–895–6471; AE, MC, V)

Continental

Art Deco treasures abound in the stunning **Restaurant Jonathan.** That molding in the second-floor Erte Room is from the old Roxy Theater, and Paradise Room corners are adorned with sculpted tropical-palm lamps from Macy's in New York. Chef Tom Cowman calls the cuisine "Continental with a Creole touch." He does delicious things with tournedos, lamb curry, and sautéed redfish, and this is the place to try the "angels on horseback" (oysters wrapped in bacon with snail butter). A new "menu for fitness" offers things like jellied chicken consommé, cayenne cucumber salad, and broiled fish, chicken, and lamb. Breads are baked right on the premises, as are the double chocolate cake, pecan pie, and almond amaretto mousse (*not* on that fitness list). This is a visual gem, with *Mobil* Four-Star and *Travel/Holiday* Awards attesting to its fine food. Chi-chi and $60 to $70. (714 North Rampart Street; 504–586–1930; all major credit cards)

The magic Brennan family touch is everywhere apparent at **Mr. B's Bistro.** The service is brisk, the surroundings charming, and the food perfectly cooked and beautifully presented. Settle back on a green leather banquette, admire the etched glass windows, and mull over a menu of everything from Eggs Creole to chopped steak to pasta. The best choices are from the hickory grill. Incidentally, if you've wanted to taste gumbo but are not keen on seafood, the gumbo ya ya is made with chicken and andouille. An informal place with soothing piano music nightly and at brunch, and a dinner bill of about $45. (201 Royal Street; 504–523–2078; all major credit cards)

Not surprisingly, the specialty at the **Rib Room** is roast prime rib of beef. However, there is a long à la carte menu, and you may have a hard time making a choice—a predicament anticipated by the thoughtful chef, who offers a *Roti-Assortis* (assortment) of prime rib, roast pork, and leg of lamb. The focal point is the rotisserie, where beef, fowl, and game sizzle over leaping flames. The decor is merrie olde England-ish, and you'll pay around $60. (Royal Orleans Hotel, 621 St. Louis Street; 504–529–5333; all major credit cards)

Get all dolled up and take lots of money to the **Sazerac Room.** This Fairmont Hotel restaurant is truly great schmaltz. A plush red velvet pouf, custom-made china, crystal, and silver on white lace cloths, and strolling musicians are all set off against a dramatic ruby background. The Sazerac has received eight consecutive *Travel/Holiday* Awards saluting its quail, duckling, steak tartare, and other specialties. Dinner for two will be about $70, but lunches are surprisingly modest, averaging $10 to $12 apiece, and there's a Dieter's Special for $11. (Incidentally, the old Roosevelt Hotel—which is now the Fairmont—bought all rights to the name "Sazerac Cocktail," created in 1859, and moved the Sazerac Bar onto its premises.) (The Fairmont Hotel at University Place; 504–529–4733; all major credit cards)

Changes are underway at Hotel Le Pavillion, and the name of its cellar restaurant is no exception. The long-time *Le Centime* is now **The Gallery,** but that may also change in the near future. One hopes that nothing whatsoever will be done to change the decor in this romantic underground spot. It's Spanish-Moorish, with white stucco walls, dark brown woodwork, and broad, dramatic arches. The menu runs all the way from frogs legs and barbecued shrimp to French onion soup to fettuccini to New York strip steak and English Grill. (This is one of the only cellars in the city.) $50 to $55. (Le Pavillion, Poydras at Baronne; 504–581–3111, ext. 7133; all major credit cards)

Totally different from the windowless romance of that cellar spot is **Le Jardin,** where broad 26-foot-high arched windows afford a romantic view of the great bend in the river and of the Quarter. Take one of the glass elevators in Canal Place, step off into the palatial pink marble lobby of the Westin Canal Place Hotel, admire the oriental rugs, giant *jardinieres,* and period furniture—and be prepared to pay a pretty price for all that opulence. The continental menu is all á la carte, and cold appetizers begin at $8.50. You can enjoy all that scenery and splendor and still remain financially solvent by coming here for the Sunday champagne brunch. It's $20 per person ($11 for the kiddies), and the Camellia Jazz Band adds nice notes. (Westin Canal Place Hotel, 100 Iberville Street; 504–566–7006; all major credit cards)

Seafood

Kabby's is not to be missed. The huge, sleek Hilton Hotel restaurant, smack on the Mississippi, is a veritable reviewing stand for the parade of ships just outside its 200-foot window. You're almost eyeball to eyeball with folks boarding the *Creole Queen*, which docks right *there*, and when the paddlewheeler begins to slip out on the river you have the giddy sensation that the restaurant rather than the boat is moving. Try the crabmeat remoulade, move on to the barbecued catfish, and keep in mind that the big slab of peanut butter pie will arrive wrapped in a rich praline sauce. A player piano entertains by day, and at night there's live music and dancing. Two can lunch for $40. Reservations suggested for dinner, especially on weekends. Casual but not funky. (Poydras Street and the river; 504–561–0500; AE, MC, V)

If the lines are too long at Galatoire's, you won't go wrong next door at **Mike Anderson's.** It's very casual, with red-and-white checkered tablecloths and lush hanging plants—but the meat of the matter is fish. Fresh South Louisiana seafood—crab, oysters, shrimp, crawfish—abounds. The "Ace" is all the catfish you can eat for $6.95. Great onion rings, hush puppies, ice-cold beer. Entrées are from $7 to $16. Casual; no reservations needed. (315 Bourbon Street; 504–524–3884; AE, MC, V)

Out around the lake the current hot ticket is **Deanie's,** which features a Family Platter for $20. The "platter" is a long-handled iron skillet piled high with enough crunchy fried sea critters to feed a family of four. A bowl of well-seasoned boiled potatoes, wearing their jackets, accompanies the entrées, and beer comes in enormous glasses. They don't take reservations and if you arrive after six on a Saturday night you'll have a long wait. (1713 Lake Avenue; 504–831–4141; AE, MC, V) **Sid-Mar's Restaurant and Lounge**, a ramshackle roadhouse in the little fishing village of Bucktown on the lake, is also usually packed with the beer- and boiled crawfish-crowd. Its screened porch is a great spot for sunset-watching. (1824 Orpheum Street; 504–831–9541; no credit cards) **Fitzgerald's** (504–282–9254; no credit cards) and **Bruning's** (504–282–9395; MC, V), both in West End Park, and the long-running **Bozo's** in Metairie (3117 21st Street; 504–831–8666; MC, V), are all dress-down dining rooms where a couple of hardcore seafood lovers can fill up for about $25.

Black ties and blue jeans mix well at **Café S'bisa** (say it *sa-bée-sah*). Bouillabaise is the specialty, and swordfish is usually on the list, along with a lot of other creatures from the sea. A casual ambience, open hearth, and piano music attract local artists and writers. A nice and easy night at about $30. (1011 Decatur Street; 504–561–8354; AE, DC, MC, V)

Muffulettas and Po-Boys

The muffuletta was "born" in 1906 in the **Central Grocery Company.** This store would be quite at home in the heart of Rome. It's a garlicky *alimentari*, with imported Italian delicacies, piles of pasta, and a butcher's case filled with prosciutto and Italian sausages. A full-scale muffuletta is $4, half is $2.50, and you can eat at the lunch counter in back or get one to go (with a Barq's root beer) and munch it on Moon Walk watching the river go by. (923 Decatur Street; 504–523–1620; no credit cards)

There are peeling sepia walls covered with pictures of its namesake and a jukebox playing only classical music in **The Napoleon House.** This very popular Quarter hangout, housed in an historic building dating from 1797, has all sorts of atmosphere, especially at night when, with its flickering candles, it is *very* romantic. In nice weather all the doors are flung wide and the tables edge out onto the sidewalk. Muffulettas, sandwiches, pastries ($3 to $7), and mixed drinks are served every day from 11 A.M. until 1 A.M. (500 Chartres Street; 504–524–9752; AE)

Ask almost any local about po-boys and they'll wax almost poetic about **Parasol's.** A rather drab neighborhood bar in the Irish Channel, Parasol's is *the* stomping ground for March 17th doings. Best known for its sloppy, drippy, and delicious roast beef, but the ham and oyster loaf are fine specimens, too. Closed Sundays and Tuesdays, and your credit card will do you no good here. (2533 Constance; 504–895–9675; no credit cards)

Hamburgers, Sandwiches & Pizza

The considerable traffic in the **Camellia Grill** is choreographed by the maitre d' who will smile you to the stool upon which you'll perch. This lunch counter, in a lovely white house right on the streetcar line, serves great burgers and inexpensive plate lunches. Its banana pie and waffles are mouthwateringly memorable. You can climb on a stool every day from 8 A.M. until 1:45 A.M., but you can't use your credit card here. (626 South Carrollton Avenue; 504–866–9573; no credit cards)

Café Maspero, across from the Jax Brewery, has a limited menu of seafood, but its main claim to fame is those oversized sandwiches. Word's been out on the street about Maspero's for a long time, and you'll have to get in line with the locals and tourists who pack the place every day except Thanksgiving and Christmas. (601 Decatur Street; 504–523–6250; no credit cards)

There are a whole lot of people who swear that the charcoal-broiled half-pound burgers at **Port of Call** are the best anywhere. There are actually two restaurants on the premises. The burgers are served in the dark side of the bar and come with baked potato, all for about $4. Open every day. (838 Esplanade; 504–523–0120; AE)

The Fatted Calf, across from Pat O'Brien's, has a campy menu and a devoted following of true believers in its burgers. The Fanny Hill is "too raw to be described," and the India Wilkes is "a *tart* combination. . . ." You can get olive-flavored burgers, burgers in burgundy sauce, burgers and caviar—all in the $4 range. A limited selection of steaks, chops, and chicken, and good mixed drinks. Very casual and cozy. (727 St. Peter; 504–523–9807; MC, V)

According to *People* magazine, **Mama Rosa's Slice of Italy** is one of the ten best pizza places in America. Prices run from $6 for a ten-inch pizza to $12 for the 14-inch "Everything Pizza." There are sandwiches made on Mama Rosa's marvelous homemade bread (you can buy a fresh loaf for $1.50), several salads, and spaghetti and meatballs for $4. You can eat in the no-frills dining room or call 523–5546 for delivery. (616 North Rampart Street; 504–523–5546; no credit cards)

There are several **Pavone's** around town making New York-style pizza. The take-out menu also includes fettuccine Alfredo ($5), spaghetti and linguine ($5 to $6), and homemade lasagna ($4.25). Pavone's

Special pizza is a 16-inch whopper for $14. Call 522–6661 for the nearest location.

American

The focal point of the Windsor Court Hotel's **Grill Room** is a $25,000 Lalique table. This elegant restaurant, with its pink marble, crystal chandeliers, Austrian shades, and stunning original artwork, is also a very comfortable room. Since the hotel's opening in 1984, the Grill Room has been a favorite of local businesspeople and has played host to visiting royalty and many a movie star. Prices on the à la carte menu are surprisingly modest, considering the opulent surroundings. Trout with lemon butter is a house specialty at $13, and the $18 filet mignon with bearnaise sauce is prepared on the mesquite charcoal grill. On Sundays the $14.50 fixed-price brunch is served with chamber music. This is the one and only restaurant in the Windsor Court and is open every day for breakfast, lunch, and dinner. (300 Gravier Street; 504–523–6000; all major credit cards)

If you'd rather not have to read a menu, go to **Winston's** in the Hilton Hotel, where it will be recited to you by a maid and butler. Settle back in a Chippendale chair, sip from imported hand-blown glassware, listen to live harp and violin music, and feast on a five-course meal in an elegant Edwardian room. Dinner only, nightly beginning at six, with changing menu and fixed price ($28.50 per person). (Hilton Hotel, 2 Poydras Street; 504–561–0500; all major credit cards)

"Miss Evelyn" Revertiga presides over the pleasant little **Honfleur,** nestled in the carriageway of the Provincial Hotel. There's a polite nod to the region with Creole gumbo, but apart from that the menu is southern fried chicken and BLT's. You can get a good breakfast for $3, and a substantial steak-and-eggs repast for $7 in this very American hideaway. A good, inexpensive departure from the richness of most other places. (1024 Chartres Street; 504–581–4995; all major credit cards)

Asian

The **Imperial Palace Regency** is a rather regal place (though the only dress stipulation is "no shorts") in the Poydras Plaza near the Superdome. There's a seven-page menu of Hunan, Szechuan, and Cantonese dishes, plus exotic drinks such as the Fog Cutter, Missionary's Downfall, and Rangoon Ruby. You can put together an Imperial Gourmet Dinner with a selection of appetizer, soup, entrée, and dessert at the entrée price plus $4.50. For starters try Hi Hop, an original Imperial Palace recipe of crabmeat, shrimp, mushrooms, and roast pork in a crisp shell. Entrees are $7 to $25. (601 Loyola; 504–522–8666; AE, MC, V)

The cuisine at **Hong Kong** is Cantonese and the view is breathtaking. It's right on the marina, with huge windows overlooking the lake and the boats tied up just outside. Inside there are red and green Chinese lanterns, an à la carte menu, and a few complete dinners including lemon chicken in a lip-puckering "secret lemon sauce." About $20. (7400 Lakeshore Drive; 504–282–1511; AE, MC, V)

Golden China is a small jewel. It's attractive without being fancy, and you get a lot for your money. There are a few Szechuan (and some American) dishes, but the menu is mostly Hunan and Cantonese, and two fine, satisfying feasts will be only about $12. This is a friendly, family-run neighborhood place with many loyal local customers. Closed Sundays. (7136 Downman Road; 504–241–8944; all major credit cards)

As can be expected in New Orleans, even **Benihana** is located in an historic French Quarter house. You can sip sake and Japanese beer in a semi-private cubicle, where your personal performing chef goes to a great deal of trouble over cutting board and hibachi. About $30, open every day. (720 St. Louis Street; 504–522–0425; all major credit cards)

If you've a yen for sushi you'll find it at **Shogun.** Besides the sushi bar there is a restaurant serving teriyaki, tempura, and such. It's open for lunch and dinner daily except Sunday and Tuesday, and you'll pay $30 to $35. (in Metairie, 1414 Veterans Boulevard; 504–833–7477; AE, MC, V)

German

The Creole influence is very strong, even in the bit of Bavaria called **Kolb's.** However, there are teutonic trappings and wiener schnitzel, and things get very oom-pah-pah during the annual Oktoberfest. Be sure and look up to see the tiny mechanical men in *lederhosen* cranking the antique ceiling fans—they are from the 1884–85 Cotton Exposition. Kolb's (pronounced kobs) is crowded with CBDers at lunch, and evenings the strolling violin and accordion duo will bring a smile to your lips. Closed Mondays. (125 St. Charles; 504–522–5079; AE, MC, V)

Mexican

Castillo's is a small room with brick walls, red tablecloths, canned Mexican music, and some of the best mole dishes around. Lots of steady customers come to Castillo's for its way above-average, very Mexican food. Appetizer prices on the luncheon menu are ridiculously low, and the combination plates are from $3.50 to $5. Couldn't be more casual; open daily from

11 A.M. until 10:30 P.M., and until midnight Friday and Saturday. (620 Conti Street; 504–523–9226; MC, V)

Across from the Old Mint, **Tortilla Flats** draws locals from the lower Quarter and the adjacent Faubourg Marigny. Piñatas are a half-hearted stab at south of the border decor, but this restaurant looks more like Texas than Mexico and the menu calls its cuisine "California Mexican." Nachos, burritos, enchiladas, etc., are served daily from 11 A.M. until 10:30 or 11 P.M.; a busy bar, attentive waiters and waitresses, and laid-back customers who pay $15 to $20 a couple complete the picture. (501 Esplanade; 504–945–9212; AE, MC, V)

The fajitas at **Café Acapulco** come sputtering and hissing on huge hot metal platters, accompanied by tortillas and liberal dollops of guacamole and pico de gallo. It's a marvelous feast. You'll see lots of families here and occasionally hear an organist. $30 to $35. Open daily, 6 A.M. to 10 or 11 P.M. (in Gretno, 932 West Bank Expressway; 504–367–7977; all major credit cards)

Italian

The menu is in Italian with English subtitles at the posh **Ristorante Pastore,** a sedate pasta emporium in the CBD. The Northern Italian dishes are served in several intimate high-ceilinged rooms of an historic building. The pasta is homemade, everything is cooked to order, and some of the dishes (including fettuccine Alfredo and angel-hair pasta asciutta) are prepared with great ceremony at your table. Put on something pretty for your $50 pasta dish. (301 Tchoupitoulas; 504–524–1122; all major credit cards)

A third generation of **Tortorici's** operates this charming place on Royal Street. It's a long narrow room with paneling and brick walls, specialties from Northern Italy, and an "Italian and Seafood Feast."

Popular with tourists, not too casual, and no credit cards. $45. (441 Royal Street; 504–523–9567; no credit cards)

Don't be put off by the flashing neon sign out front. **Toney's Spaghetti House** is not a Bourbon Street rip-off. It's a simple, unpretentious restaurant where the pasta is called spaghetti and comes with meatballs. Toney's bills itself as a "Creole-Italian" place, and there are other things besides pizza, antipasto, and parmigiana. A family place, open from 7 A.M. until just after midnight every day except Sunday. (210 Bourbon Street; 504–568–9556; AE, MC, V)

Steakhouses

The **Crescent City Steak House** set the local steak style more than 50 years ago. New Orleans steaks are broiled in butter sauce and come to you still cooking on hot metal platters. There isn't much to be said about the decor in this restaurant, but you may want to write home about the food. Open all day, Tuesday through Sunday, and you can come casual. $50. (1001 North Broad; 504–821–3271; all major credit cards)

Pro-football players and politicians pounce on the aged U.S. Prime beef at **Ruth's Chris Steak House.** The menu is à la carte, the steak fries are great, and the salad is a meal in itself. Both locations are casual places, both are open seven days a week, and the tab will be about $50. (711 North Broad; 504–482–9278; also at 3633 Veterans Boulevard; 504–888–3600; all major credit cards)

You CAN Take It With You . . .

If you get hooked on New Orleans food (you won't be the first), and want to learn to make some of the dishes at home, check into the **New Orleans School of Cooking.** Classes are not hands-on, but you do get your teeth into things after watching the chef-lecturer prepare jambalaya, crawfish étouffée, pecan pie, or red beans and rice. It's an everyday affair, from 10:00 A.M. until 1:00 P.M., and costs $15 per person. When you call to make the necessary reservation, ask what's on the agenda for the day you want to attend. The school is behind the retail shop, where you can buy cookbooks, Cajun spices, and a wide variety of local delicacies. (New Orleans School of Cooking, Jax Brewery, 620 Decatur Street; 504–525–2665; AE, MC)

Health Food

New Orleans is not a city in which to find bean sprouts on every block. There are a few health food places, however, among them **Back to the Garden,** in the Quarter. It's a small room with a huge mural showcasing deep-purple grapes and a menu offering Stir-Fried Veggies ($5), avocado-and-cheese sandwiches ($3), quiche, salad, and so forth. For dessert try the "Awful Waffle," made with wheat and topped with frozen honey yogurt and fresh fruit ($3), or go for the $2 bread pudding. Very, very laid-back. (207 Dauphine; 504–524–6915; no credit cards)

Nightlife

Unless you've lived most of your life on Mars, you're aware that jazz was born right here in New Orleans. But if you're a first-timer here, you'll probably be astonished—most visitors are—at the sounds of the city. New Orleans's music is not exactly tucked away in a backroom somewhere. It sizzles out into the streets from clubs all over the Quarter. Stroll down Bourbon Street any night—or noon—and hear throbbing R&B, ragin' Cajun, honky-tonking player pianos, guitars, ghetto-blasters backing up breakdancers, banjos, Irish folks songs—even an occasional bagpipe. Down on Moon Walk you'll often see a lone trumpeter, silhouetted against the river. Nine-piece Dixieland bands pop up behind a dropped hat in Jackson Square, mournful saxophonists wail everywhere, and there are exuberant musicians beating out rhythms on homemade instruments much like those of the old-time "spasm" bands that used to play in the streets of old Storyville.

Pick up a copy of the weekly newspaper *Gambit* and check its excellent calendar to find out who's playing where. And Frances Fernandez of the New Orleans Jazz Club (504–455–6847) has a wealth of information about the local jazz doings. There are several Ticketmaster outlets around town, and you can call 504–888–8181 to find out about theater and other entertainment events.

New Orleans is one of the few 24-hour towns in the country. A given club may not necessarily be open around the clock, but there are no legal closing times and some bars never close. (If you call to ask what time a place closes, you may get a cheery, "How late would you *like* us to stay open?"). You can buy package liquor any hour of the day or night in liquor, grocery, and drug stores. (The well-stocked Royal Street A&P, at the corner of Royal and St. Peter in the Quarter, never closes.)

As we go to press, the legal drinking age here is 18, but that may soon be legislated up to 21. And even now there are a few places that won't sell to anyone under age 21.

And speaking of imbibing, some of the libations indigenous to the Crescent City will knock your socks off. The Hurricane, created at Pat O'Brien's, is a sweetly potent concoction of passionfruit and rum. (Legend has it that its birth was accidental, the result of a supplier's having delivered an unseemly quantity of rum and fruit juice to the bar.) The original Sazerac Cocktail was made with bourbon, bitters, absinthe, and Sazerac brandy. It's said that this drink was the first cocktail, originated by a Monsieur Peychaud in a French Quarter bar. He served his *coquetiers* to his customers, who anglicized the name to "cocktail," in about 1859. Only the bourbon and bitters remain from the original recipe, but this baby is not for the faint of heart. The Ramos Gin Fizz is made with egg whites, orange flower water, cream, soda, and gin.

You won't find a drink at **Preservation Hall,** and unless you get there early you won't find a place to sit either. No booze, no food, no smoking, no air conditioning, no comfy chairs and tables, neither stage, mike, sound system, nor cutesy emcees. Nothing in the hall at all, except for the best traditional jazz and Dixieland on the face of the earth. All of the jazz greats play here, a different group every night, young and old, white and black. One night you may hear the Humphrey Brothers (Willie on clarinet, band leader Percy on trumpet), Sing Miller on piano, Narvin Kimball on banjo, or Frank Demond on trombone. You'll hear Wendell Brunois, one of the most talented young trumpet players around, and John Royen, who almost takes the piano apart. Kid Sheik is here, putting his trumpet down for a joyful vocal on "them Saints," and the incomparable Emanuel Sayles, still a dynamo on the banjo at age 75. The gate opens every night at eight o'clock, and the music stomps off half an hour later. Get in line at 7:30, and make sure you're in the hall line: Pat O'Brien's is next door, and you can get lost in the crunch. (Stop at Pat's and take out a Hurricane. You can take the paper cup into the hall.) Drop two bucks in the basket at the gate, go through the carriageway and turn left into probably the grungiest room you've ever seen. There are a few crude benches, some cushions on the floor, which would benefit greatly from a bath and from which you could shine the shoes of the music-makers, and standing room. The hall is not for earthly comforts; it's for your soul. (726 St. Peter Street; daytime phone 504–522–2238, nighttime phone 504–523–8939; no credit cards)

There's a whole other show at **Pat O'Brien's,** next door. As you go through the carriageway, there's a bar to the left of you, a pretty patio bar in front of you, and a bar to the right of you. The entertainment is in that largest, liveliest bar to the right—where the pianos are. The term "piano bar" usually conjures up images of sleek creatures draped over an ebony grand and dreamily listening to late-night torch songs. Well, scratch everything but "grand," "late-night" and "songs." This is a raucous, sing-along, shout-along place, where talented teams of female pianists pound out every song ever written, and their specialties are "state" songs. They holler out, "Where'r y'all from?"

and then start singing "The Eyes of Texas," "California, Here I Come," "On Wisconsin," and so forth. Pat's is a fun place, and those 29-ounce Hurricanes contribute to the merriment. It's open every day from 10 A.M. until 4:00 A.M. (5:00 A.M. on Fridays and Saturdays), and there's no cover charge. (718 St. Peter Street; 504–525–4823; no credit cards)

Just up the street you can hang out on the corner of St. Peter and Bourbon and listen to the music pouring out of **Maison Bourbon, Bayard's Jazz Alley, Mo' Jazz,** and **Krazy Korner.** You won't have any trouble at all hearing it. Pick a sound that appeals to you and go inside—drinks are usually around $5—or just lean against the lamppost and listen away.

The doors open at noon, seven days a week, at **The Absinthe Bar,** but around midnight is when the music—R&B and hard-driving progressive jazz—really begins to move. Locals hang out here till the break of dawn. No cover, but there is a two-drink minimum. (400 Bourbon Street; 504–525–8108; AE)

The **Seaport Café** is a two-story bar and restaurant with a Bourbon Street balcony and the songs of Sally Townes. The food is Cajun and Creole—mostly seafood—and the mood is usually pretty merry. Sally sings from 9:00 P.M. until 1 A.M. Thursday through Saturday, and the Cat's Meow joins her Sunday afternoons from 3 P.M. until 6 P.M. (424 Bourbon Street; 504–568–0981; all major credit cards)

The loudest sounds you'll hear at the corner of Bourbon and Toulouse are coming out of the **Landmark Hotel.** There's a lot going on inside the place, which is on the site of the old French Opera House. A pianist/vocalist works very hard in the lounge, and later a trio takes over the entertainment chores. The Reunion Café serves meals cafeteria-style around the clock on Fridays and Saturdays. (The Landmark Ho-

tel, 541 Bourbon Street; 504–524–7611; all major
credit cards)

Lulu White's Mahogany Hall takes its name from
one of the better known bordellos of the notorious old
Storyville. It's now the home of the famous Dukes of
Dixieland, who alternate with a great female vocalist
named Banu Gibson. Lulu's is a great Dixieland place,
with show times at 9:00, 10:20, and 11:40 P.M. (ask
about cover charges and such when you call for reservations). Sports fans will appreciate Monday Night
Football on the giant television screen. (309 Bourbon
Street; 504–525–5595; CB, DC, MC. V)

They've been going strong at **The Famous Door**
for ages and ages. There's continuous music from
8:00 P.M. on from the bandstand behind the bar, and
in the doorway waiters and waitresses in straw hats
and perpetual motion keep up with the beat. You can
hear almost anything here, from R&B to progressive
to country-western. (339 Bourbon Street; 504–522–
7626; AE)

The **Can-Can Cabaret** in the Royal Sonesta is
pretty corny, but it's harmless (there are usually families with small kids in the house), and for ten bucks you
can have a drink and see a lot of legs and ruffles.
Things are infinitely more sophisticated, soothing,
and romantic in the Sonesta's **Mystick Den,** where a
classical guitarist does three shows nightly. (300 Bourbon Street; 504–568–0300; all major credit cards)

Across the street from the French Market, **The
New Storyville Jazz Club** showcases local talent, such
as Luther Kent & Trick Bag and Chris Burke's group,
as well as big-timers like Buddy Rich and Leon Rus-
sell. Weeknights things rev up at 8:00 (unless there's
a "name" headliner, in which case showtime is 10),
and you're welcome to drop in any time after 1:00 on
Sunday afternoons. There's food as well as drink here,
with breakfast available anytime at $4 to $7. Appetiz-

ers include a shot glass of Oyster Cocktail for 40 cents, burgers are $4 to $5, a six-ounce rib-eye with onion rings is $8, and the house specialty—a Mug of Bouillabaise with French bread—costs less than $4. This is a really fun place, with a capacity of about 500, and you can bring the kids along. Call first to ask about the lineup and admission charge. (1104 Decatur Street; 504–525–8199; AE, DC)

Down along the fringe of the Quarter, **Snug Harbor** has a nautical motif and mostly young folks who turn out in droves to hear local favorites such as the Pfister Sisters and the David Torkanowski Trio. The Pfisters (pronounced fisters) are a trio of unrelated ladies who put on a terrific act which includes Andrews Sisters' standards, torch songs, and show tunes. You can have dinner in the adjoining restaurant (burgers $4 or $5, steaks $15) before going in to catch the show (admission charge at the door is $3 to $5). It's open every day from 4 P.M. until 1 or 2 A.M. (626 Frenchman Street; 504–949–0696; AE)

A bit further downriver, in Faubourg Marigny, **Feelings Café D'Aunoy** has a rather stylish dining room serving Creole specialties and a courtyard serving up entertainment. Songstress Lady B.J. is sometimes on the bill, or you might catch a flamboyant gay revue complete with glittering costumes and outrageous wigs. Feelings is usually packed with locals having a great time, every night of the week. (If you have dinner here, be sure to leave space for the justly famous peanut butter pie.) (2600 Chartres Street; 504–945–2222; MC, V)

The Esplanade Lounge, in the marbled halls of the Royal Orleans, is an opulent spot to have a few drinks and listen to sophisticated piano music. (621 St. Louis; 504–529–5333; all major credit cards)

For ages and ages the Dukes of Dixieland were "at home" at Duke's Place atop the Monteleone Hotel.

Now the Dukes are at Lulu White's, and **Duchess Place** features the Sylvia Johns Trio. This is a terrific hotel club, and there'll be special doings to celebrate the Monteleone's 100th birthday in 1986. You'll need a reservation. (214 Royal Street; 504–523–3341; all major credit cards)

Chances are you grew up listening to late-night radio broadcasts "coming to you live from **The Blue Room** of the Roosevelt Hotel in downtown New Orleans." Well, the Roosevelt's now the Fairmont, but the famous old supper club is still going strong. You can dine and dance to the big-band sounds of Herb Tassin, and listen to the likes of Tony Bennett, the Ink Spots, Joel Grey, or Frank Sinatra. The club opens for dinner at 7 P.M., and weeknights there's a $35 per person dinner-and-show package. By all means drape yourself in something grand and paint the Blue Room red. Closed Sunday. Call for reservations and further info about cover and entertainment charges. (The Fairmont Hotel at University Place; 504–529–7111; AE, DC, MC, V)

There are hot licks in the splendid center lobby of the Hotel Meridien, scene of **Le Jazz Meridien** every night but Sunday. Professor P's piano music begins at 5:30 P.M., and at 9 P.M. you can hear the Louisiana Repertory Jazz Ensemble, New Orleans Classic Jazz Orchestra, Joe Lastie Jr. and his New Orleans Jazz Band, the Creole Rice Band, or Razzberrie Ragtimers Jazz Band. No cover for a lot of great jazz. (614 Canal Street; 504–525–6500; all major credit cards)

At the foot of Poydras Street down by the river there is a virtual city of music within the Hilton Hotel. First of all, **Pete Fountain's** place is here, in a big red velvet room with wrought-iron railings on the third level. You really shouldn't be allowed to leave the city without hearing New Orleans's internationally known native son. The club is not Pete Fountain's in name only: this is the man's *home*, and he's here Tuesday through Saturday at 10 P.M. The $16.50 charge includes one drink and incomparable clarinet music. Reservations necessary. Up on the 29th floor, the

Rainforest is a jam-packed disco in a tropical "rainforest" setting. There's an intermittent Sound and Light Show, with simulated crackling thunder and flashing lightning, and down below the river's a silken ribbon rolled out over the horizon. Over in the riverside part of the hotel, you can dance to live music at **Kabby's,** a huge, stunning place with one of the best river views in town. All three nightspots are located in the Hilton Hotel #2 Poydras Street; 504–523–4374; AE only. (Pete Fountain's); 504–561–0500, all major credit cards (Rainforest and Kabby's).

Nearby and 33 floors up, you can ride around town in the slowly revolving **Top of the Mart** lounge. (Don't put anything on the windowsill; it doesn't go along for the ride.) There's a one-drink minimum, no food, and the Smart Guys Combo jazzes things up on weekends. (ITM Building, 2 Canal Street; 504–522–9795; no credit cards)

There are satisfying New Orleans sounds in the veddy British **Windsor Court Hotel.** Sink down in a cushy chair in Le Salon and have "Jazz and Champagne" with the John Mahoney Jazz Trio, Thursday through Saturday from 10 P.M. until 1 A.M. You can hear the Joel Simpson Duo nightly until 11:30 P.M. in the Grill Bar, and jazz pianist Marci Noonan can be heard from time to time in the lobby lounge. (300 Gravier; 504–523–6000; all major credit cards)

No doubt about it, there's nothing more romantic than a moonlight dinner-plus-jazz riverboat cruise. The gigantic *President* plies the waters every Friday and Saturday night from 8 until 11 P.M. (you board at 7 P.M. at the Canal Street dock). Cost is $10 for the cruise (you can buy dinner, snacks, and cocktails on board), and there's ample dancing space on this four-decker. Call 504–524–7245 for info about the *President*'s special concert cruises, and 504–522–3030 about its moonlight and Sunday brunch cruises. The *Creole Queen* glitters out on the river, and for $26 per person you get an incredible buffet of Creole food (there's a cash bar) and dancing to a live Dixieland band. The *Creole Queen*'s berth is also at the Canal

Street landing. Call 504–524–0814 to find out more about cruising aboard this $4 million beauty. The 265-foot *Natchez* slips away from the Toulouse Street Wharf every night at 6:30 for two hours of toe-tapping music and Mississippi River nostalgia. It begins boarding thirty minutes before departure, at $11.50 for adults, half that for children under twelve (cruise only; dinner plus cruise is $24, children half-price), but the fun starts as soon as you get within hearing distance of the paddlewheeler's loud, wheezy, and off-key calliope. More info at 504–586–8777 or 504–587–0734.

Tipitina's is back in business at its old Uptown stomping grounds, having reopened in early 1986 with great hoopla. As we go to press it's too early to tell if "Tips" will live up to its legend, but there are a lot of folks who wish it well. Sounds bursting out of this cavernous club could be reggae or rock, New Wave or old-time jazz, all depending upon who's on stage, but you can count on a lively crowd and fun extending into the wee hours. The late "Professor Longhair" loved to play "Tips," and so did the Neville Brothers, Dr. John, and a host of other local favorites. (501 Napolean; 504–895–8477; no credit cards)

The **Maple Leaf Bar** is always crowded with students from nearby Tulane and Loyola universities. You can get two-for-one drinks from 9:00 P.M. until the 10 P.M. showtime (the music bill changes nightly but it's always live), and there's a cover charge of $2 to $3 weeknights, $4 to $5 on weekends. There are huge pitchers of beer, chess players hunkered down on the enclosed patio, dancing on a floor the size of your big toenail, and a guaranteed good time. (8316 Oak Street; 504–866–9359; no credit cards)

Another popular Uptown hangout is **Tyler's Beer Garden,** where the music is live Tuesday through Saturday (cover $4 or $5) and oysters come a dime apiece. You may hear the James Rivers Movement,

Germain Bazzle with the Ellis Marsalis Trio, or the John Mooney Louisiana Band. (5234 Magazine Street; 504–891–4989; AE, DC, MC, V)

Yuppies love dancing the night away at **Forty-One Forty-One.** There are dance floor and bars, upstairs and down, and a huge canopied patio in the rear. It opens at 3:00 P.M. and closes in the wee hours. (4139 St. Charles Avenue; 504–891–9873; AE, MC, V)

If you're more in tune with classical music, the **New Orleans Symphony** performs November through March in the Orpheum Theatre. The Orpheum is at 129 University Place, across from the Fairmont Hotel, and the phone number is 504–525–0500. The **New Orleans Opera** season begins around the first of October. Performances are in the Theatre for the Performing Arts, adjacent to the Quarter, and you can find out more from the New Orleans Opera Association, 333 St. Charles Avenue, 504–529–2278.

National touring companies of Broadway hits can be seen at the **Saenger Theatre.** It's at 143 North Rampart, at the corner of Canal, and the number to call for its news is 504–524–2490.

New Orleans is a great city for community theater. In fact, its **Le Petit Theatre du Vieux Carre,** housed in an historic building on Jackson Square, is the oldest continuously operating community theater in America. The **Contemporary Arts Center,** near Lee Circle, houses an interesting art gallery and presents contemporary, sometimes avant-garde, plays. The **Theatre Marigny** is a pocket-sized place doing a lot of good work, and there are three dinner theaters in town—the **Rose, Minacapelli's,** and the **Bonaparte. Tulane, Loyola** and the **University of New Orleans** all have community theaters, and **Uno's Lakefront Arena** often presents headliners like Frank Sinatra.

And remember, the traditional nightcap is café au lait and beignets at **Café du Monde** (see *Dining*) in Jackson Square.

Festivals

Mardi Gras

Every year on January 6, the St. Charles Streetcar is commandeered by the Phunny Phorty Phellows (and a phew phemales). Festooned with balloons, blaring with jazz bands, the streetcar takes the Phellows for a rollicking ramble up the avenue. On that day, bakeries all over town display king cakes (wreath-shaped coffee cakes frosted in Mardi Gras colors). That night the Twelfth Night Revelers have their annual ball. It is, after all, Twelfth Night. Carnival season has officially begun.

A few days later, a police escort with wailing sirens leads a whole fleet of white Eldorado convertibles through the Quarter. The Bards of Bohemia are headed for a banquet at the Court of Two Sisters. Later, dressed in fanciful costumes and armed with beads, they board floats, mount horses, or climb into horse-drawn carriages for the parade which will take them to

Municipal Auditorium for their annual Carnival festivities.

The Mardi Gras colors of purple, green, and gold begin to appear on balconies. Banners, streamers, balloons, masks, bunting—a few more appear every day. By the end of January, almost every balcony in the Quarter is decorated with something gold, green, and purple.

By the time the krewes (social organizations which celebrate Carnival with elaborate parades and balls) start rolling, Carnival fever is running high. As the days tick off toward the last big day, more and more krewes take to the streets, parading along established routes throughout the city. There are major parades every one of the 11 days before Fat Tuesday (the literal translation of "Mardi Gras"), and in the final four days Carnival fever bursts into total madness. There are several parades every day and every night, and nonstop partying. New Orleans on Fat Tuesday is not to be believed.

New Orleans's Mardi Gras parades are not your average parades. For one thing, the floats are absolutely spectacular: extravagant marvels of gigantic papier-mâché gorillas, castles, dragons, antebellum houses, politicians, whatever. There is no central theme for Mardi Gras (nor is there a central organizing committee). Each krewe adopts its own theme, a different one every year, with each float decorated in some manifestation of the main "storyline." There are anywhere from 15 to 35 or 40 floats in a parade, some of them double-deckers, some of them carrying jazz bands. Most of the floats carry masked krewe members in elaborate satins and sequins, all of them winding up and zinging throws, or trinkets, out to a shrieking mob along the route.

If there is any one thing that makes Mardi Gras parades here unique it's the throws. These souvenir trinkets—plastic beads, doubloons (decorated aluminum "coins"), plastic cups, spears, and a variety of other things—are tossed to overeager spectators shouting, "Throw me somethin' mister." Throws have been a tradition since the Twelfth Night Revelers parade of 1879, and different kinds appear every year. Ever since they were first tossed in 1960, the doubloons have been the most coveted. But the beads are the most displayed. In the last couple of weeks of Carnival you see thousands of them all over town: strung up on lampposts, dripping off balconies, swinging off motorcycles, and on almost every neck in the city. Everybody wears beads—waitresses, concierges, puppies, musicians. They're worn proudly, like Purple Heart medals.

For the crowds along the routes, the parades are not spectator events. They are contact sports. Hand to hand combat. Bagging beads and doubloons is what it's all about. As the trinkets shower down from the masquers on the floats, the crowd goes nuts, yelling, snatching, and stomping. A lady in a slinky white satin gown will grapple with a kid in jeans and sneakers for a single strand of cheap plastic beads which both of them are already loaded down with. People sit on other people's shoulders or climb up on lampposts to get a better shot at the treasures. Others don't mess with amateur tactics. They bring stepladders and butterfly nets. And the thrill is in the capture. The person who spent fifteen minutes standing on somebody's shoulders to snag beads dangling from a balcony will probably give them to a total stranger with a "Happy Mardi Gras." Incidentally, as regards the doubloons—when they come showering through the air and clank on the pavement clever strategists know to stomp on one first and establish possession before stretching a bare hand down to pick it up.

Two other special ingredients of Mardi Gras parades here are the flambeau carriers and the marching bands. Flambeaux are tall torches, fueled by kerosene and carried by men wearing white hoods and white robes. In the 19th century they were the only means of illumination during the night parades. Only six of the 50 or so krewes feature the flambeau carriers now. Three that do are Hermes, Proteus, and Comus, all of which parade in the final days. If you're here for Carnival don't miss the flambeau carriers—they are a sight to behold as they come dancing down the street. As for the marching bands, they come from all over the country but you have not seen strutting until you've seen one of New Orleans's own high-stepping high school bands jazz it up. They really get down and put on a great show.

Two parades not to be missed are Endymion and Bacchus. The 1,100-member Endymion rolls out the Saturday night before Fat Tuesday. It's one of the splashiest of the Carnival parades with about 35 or so floats and a celebrity grand marshall. The glittery parade winds up at the Superdome for its annual Extravaganza, which about 11,000 people buy tickets to attend. The Bacchus krewe marches the next night, also with a celebrity monarch. Bob Hope, Henry Winkler, Pete Fountain, and Ron Howard are among those who have appeared as the Greek god of wine in the spectacular parade. Bacchus parades through downtown and on into the Rivergate, floats and all, for its big bash.

Things get moving very early Mardi Gras morning (if they ever stopped the night before) with the appearance, at about 7:00 A.M., of several different "walking clubs." The Jefferson City Buzzards, the Marching Fools, and—the best-known—Pete Fountain's Half-Fast Walking Club, with Pete in his white suit and white cape, playing his clarinet, are among the ones that ramble around town. These are not what you would call snappy drill teams. They straggle around with dixieland bands, making frequent stops to refuel in bars along the way and handing out crepe paper flowers to ladies in exchange for a kiss.

The first major event Mardi Gras morning is the parade of the black Zulu Social Aid & Pleasure Club. In 1949, it was Louis Armstrong who made King Zulu's traditional trip downriver on the *Cotton Blossom*.

The king's annual arrival is scheduled for 8:00 A.M., but schedules mean little during Carnival. With an honor guard of Soulful Warriors and an entourage including the outlandish likes of Big Shot, Witch Doctor, and Mr. Big Stuff, Zulu makes his way up Canal Street. It isn't the floats that make this parade a must-see. Zulu began parading in 1909 as a spoof on Rex, and krewe members, gotten up in grass skirts and all manner of weird gear, carry on the tradition of outrageousness. Zulu souvenirs are among the most coveted—gilded coconuts, bikinis, umbrellas, tambourines, and black medallion beads. (You might want to keep an eye out for flying spears.)

About a million people jam the streets by the time the Monarch of Carnival makes his appearance around noon. What began in 1872 as a hastily gotten up parade to entertain the Grand Duke Alexis Alexandrovich Romanov is now one of the most splendid spectacles of Carnival. The duke visited the city during Mardi Gras, and at that time the only Carnival parade in New Orleans was the night parade of the Mistick Krewe of Comus. The Rex parade was a daytime affair to extend the festivities honoring the royal Russian. The purple, gold, and green of the first Rex cavalcade became the traditional Carnival colors, and the Mardi Gras theme is the song which was played by its marching bands. "If Ever I Cease to Love" was sung by an actress named Lydia Thompson in the musical comedy *Bluebeard.* The duke had attended the play in New York, and by all accounts he was smitten with the lady. At the time of the duke's visit to New Orleans, the lady and the play were here also. Local bands learned the schmaltzy song, and played it over and over as the Rex parade passed the duke on the reviewing stand.

Mounted on a white stallion, the Rex captain leads the parade, followed by 32 krewe lieutenants, all on horseback and garbed in colorful costumes with

flowing capes and helmets with high billowy plumes.
Rex himself, resplendent in shining finery, rides on a
float complete with throne and giant canopy of purple
and gold. There are jazz bands blaring "If Ever I
Cease to Love," and about 350 masquers having a fine
time aboard 25 floats. This parade is not to be missed.

Although the next formal parade is not until
night, the cavalcade on Canal Street continues with
the truck parades that follow Rex. Elaborately decorated flatbed trucks loaded with costumed revelers
famous for their generosity in the throwing department ease along through the throng. Canal at this
point is one mad amorphous critter with a million
waving arms and an insatiable appetite. If you're on
Canal at Carondelet, you'll see the costumed com-
mentators of WDSU-TV attempting to do a live play-
by-play for the shut-ins while being pelted by beads
and trinkets. They sit on an exposed platform, sitting
ducks for the truckers who get an annual bang out of
beaning the "Six O'Clock News" team.

Meanwhile, there is a great deal going on in the
Quarter. There are a lot of costumed masquers among
the Canal Street revelers, but the most fantastic outfits
are to be seen in the French Quarter. There are walking crayons, trash cans, and firecrackers, and any number of historical, cartoon, and literary characters.
Some of the costumes are scruffy, but many of them
are elaborate delectations costing several thousand
dollars. Far and away the most dazzling are the ones
worn in the annual gay competitions in the Quarter.
The display of plumed headdresses, glittering sequins, and ermine-trimmed robes makes the average
Las Vegas showgirl look prim. You won't have any
trouble finding one of the contests. They're enor-
mously popular and always draw a huge crowd.

The Mistick Krewe of Comus is traditionally the
last to parade because it was Comus that began the
tradition of parading in New Orleans. Creole New
Orleanians celebrated Carnival with lavish *bals masques*
(masked balls), but the only "parades" were little
more than street riots. In 1857, in a men's club over

the old Gem Bar at 127 Royal Street, a group of men from Mobile, Alabama, met and formed the Secret Society of Comus. Mobile, also a Creole colony, *did* celebrate Carnival with parades, and the transplanted Alabamans decided that their adopted city should do the same. Adopting the name of the Greek god of revelry, the merry men from Mobile coined the word "krewe," and organized the first of New Orleans's famed parades. While Rex, the King of Carnival, is always a well-known civic leader, the identity of King Comus is never revealed. The Mistick Krewe of Comus continues its tradition of secrecy.

With only about 15 floats, the oldest krewe parade is one of the smallest. But it is always exciting, partly because of the flambeaux, partly because of Comus, in mask and plumed cap, holding his golden goblet. This parade more than any other epitomizes the mystique of Mardi Gras.

In Municipal Auditorium just before midnight, the king and queen of Comus meet Rex and his queen for the closing ceremonies of Carnival. The meeting of the two courts is televised each year by WDSU-TV, and if you can tear yourself off the celebrating streets you can see a dazzling half hour of make-believe pageantry. You almost need to wear sunglasses to counteract the glare of so many regal robes, gowns, and crowns.

At midnight, a cavalcade of mounted police, motorcycles, and police cars begins slowly maneuvering down Bourbon Street. Police with megaphones politely inform the wildly celebrating throng, "Mardi Gras is over." The procession is a slow one. Nobody wants to stop partying. But at the stroke of midnight Fat Tuesday ushers in Ash Wednesday and the beginning of Lent. And Mardi Gras really is over.

As for where to best see the parades, all of the downtown krewes march on Canal Street and St.

Charles Avenue, and the ones whose Carnival balls are at Municipal Auditorium in Armstrong Park turn on Rampart Street. The thickest crowds are on Canal and St. Charles, and you can sometimes see the parades better on Rampart. But there's no "best place" to see or to bag trinkets. The masquers may have thrown all of their throws by the time they reach the end of the line—or they may shower the crowd with souvenirs in a final grand gesture. There's no way to tell. You can usually make a bigger catch by standing a few feet back from the line of march. Some of those guys really heave the beads. On the other hand, if you're right behind a police barricade you're positioned to zip out into the street and scoop up stray beads off the pavement. With a couple of parades under your belt you can map out your own strategy.

As Pete Fountain has said, "You just can't describe Mardi Gras to anyone. You try to tell people what it's like, but they just don't understand. Not unless they've been here and seen it for themselves."

If you plan to come for Mardi Gras, by all means get a copy of Arthur Hardy's *Mardi Gras Guide.* The little paperback costs $3.50 and includes everything you need to know about the greatest free show on earth—parade dates and routes, krewe histories, current "most coveted throw" info, everything. You can order it from Arthur Hardy & Associates, Box 8058, New Orleans 70182, or you can pick one up from any newsstand in town.

Since Mardi Gras is 46 days before Easter, it can fall anywhere from early February to early March. For your planning information, Mardi Gras will be on March 3, 1987, and February 16, 1988.

Jazz & Heritage Festival

The Jazz & Heritage Festival has been getting bigger and bigger each year since it snuck up on the celebration scene in the late 1960s. More than 3,000 musicians, famous and fledgling, come from all over the world now to take part in the internationally acclaimed Jazz Fest, with thousands of people pouring into town to hear them.

The ten-day celebration occurs in late April or early May, with the heaviest action out at the Fairgrounds Racetrack the weekends at the beginning and the end of the festival. Tents set up in the racetrack infield resound with reggae, gospel, R&B, C&W, Cajun, traditional jazz, blues—the works. And you won't go hungry out there either. Food tents dish out plenty of red beans & rice, jambalaya, shrimp, po-boys, fried chicken, and fried alligator tails. In still other tents, artisans display handmade leather, wood, jewelry and other crafts. That time of the year the mercury matches the hot sounds. It's definitely short-shorts time.

The music is not by any means confined to the Fairgrounds. This is a 24-hour town even without special events. On any night during the Jazz Fest you can stop in some little bar on Bourbon at 9 P.M., stagger out 12 hours later, and the music will, probably, still be going strong. There are concerts on the *President*, at Municipal Auditorium—all over town. Musicians "sit in" in dingy bars, jam in courtyards, play on street corners. This really is ten days of flat-out music.

Don't worry if you don't have a car. Special shuttle buses join the regular city buses to ferry folks to and from the Fairgrounds. Round-trip tickets for the shuttles include admission to the Fairgrounds.

For further information, write to the Jazz and Heritage Festival, Box 2530, 1205 North Rampart Street, New Orleans 70176.

Spring Fiesta

As noted previously, Spring Fiesta is a lovely time for a visit, especially a first visit. New Orleans is all blossomed out in its tropical finery. It's warm but not yet scorching: all in all a great time of year here.

The 19-day fiesta begins the first Friday evening after Easter. It is ushered in by a romantic parade through the French Quarter. Called "A Night in Old New Orleans," the pretty procession is of horse-drawn carriages carrying ladies in hoop skirts and men in old-fashioned frock coats. Antique cars, mounted posse clubs, and, of course, marching bands complete the parade. Many private homes are open for the fiesta tours, including houses in the French Quarter, the Garden District, and plantation homes on the Great River Road. Costumed hosts and hostesses greet visitors and talk about the historical significance of their homes, tell anecdotes, and so forth. Don't miss the Patios by Candlelight tours: anyone of a nostalgic bent will have a hard time leaving town after one of those. For dates and tour descriptions, write Spring Fiesta, 826 St. Ann Street, New Orleans 70116.

Other Festivals

This being a city geared for good times, you'll find something going on almost any time you come. Apart from August, which is a resting and roasting month, the calendar is full of activities.

The Lenten season is twice temporarily interrupted here, once on March 17 by the Irish and again two days later by the Italians. The Irish Channel is the main drag of the annual St. Patrick's Day parades, with Parasol's the headquarters for the wearers of the green. St. Joseph's Day, March 19, is a major festival for the city's vast Italian population, most of whom are Sicilian. Some of their homes are open to display the elaborate altars piled high with food. The Saturday after St. Joseph's Day there is a parade through the French Quarter. Another big annual Italian festival is *Festa d'Italia,* a week-long celebration of the birth of Christopher Columbus. The second Monday in October, Piazza d'Italia on Poydras Street is transformed into an old-fashioned Italian square. There is music, dancing, lots of food to be sampled, parades, and, usually, celebrities on hand. A big crowd always turns out to help the Italians celebrate their heritage.

The French Quarter Festival will be three years old in April of 1986, and if it keeps on growing it will be to Jackson Square what the Jazz Fest is to the Fairgrounds. Many of the famous restaurants set up food booths on the grass of the former parade grounds in the Square. Needless to say, there is music everywhere. The FQF is usually held on one of the first weekends in April.

The focus is on food here every day of the year, and in the summertime there are two events which spotlight the city's culinary triumphs. The New Orleans Food Festival tempts epicures and torments dieters annually on the last weekend before the Fourth of July. The two-day Food Fest is at the Rivergate, where chefs from 40 or 50 restaurants exhibit their specialties, tasting portions of which are 75 cents to $1.75. The finale of the festival is a gala seven-course gourmet dinner at one of the best restaurants. Tickets for the black-tie affair are $60 per person. The second event is *La Fête,* the National Festival of Food and Cookery, which runs for the entire month of July and which is exactly what the name suggests. *La Fête* emphasizes Creole and Cajun food in various activities around town. Also in July, a Bastille Day celebration salutes the city's French connection.

The big New Year's Eve bash in Jackson Square is on the network television line-up of New Year's Eve blowouts. It wouldn't be New Orleans without a parade to get things going, and thousands of people jam the square to watch the ball drop from atop the Jax Brewery. The revelers are joined by the thousands who've come to town for the annual Sugar Bowl game in the Superdome, always a major event. And the dust has not yet settled when the Phunny Phorty Phellows board the Streetcar again and Carnival season is once again underway. . . .

Excursions Outside of Town

The Great River Road, which hugs the Mississippi between New Orleans and Baton Rouge, is decorated with grand old antebellum plantations. Many are open to the public, and several are clustered fairly close together about an hour's drive to the west of the city. There being two banks of the river, there are two river roads, which travel along the way under aliases, such as highways 44 and 48 on the East Bank and 18 on the West Bank. What with refineries and such, the Great River Road ain't what it used to be. Restored to former grandeur, the plantations *are*.

Destrehan, closest to New Orleans (eight miles west of the New Orleans International Airport on the River Road; 504–763–9315) is the oldest intact plantation in the lower Mississippi Valley. The simple West Indies-style house was built in 1787 by a "free man of color," and a later owner added the Greek Doric columns. It houses a collection of European and early

American antiques. About 20 minutes from it, west along the River Road, **San Francisco** looks like a frilly riverboat run aground. The Steamboat Gothic house was the setting for the novel of that title by Frances Parkinson Keyes. Completed in about 1856, San Francisco is an ornate three-story mansion with two graceful exterior staircases, stunning ceiling frescoes, and exquisite furnishings. **Houmas House** (located near the junction of highways 22 and 44 in Burnside; 504–473–7841) was the setting for the movie, *Hush, Hush, Sweet Charlotte,* and for the pilot film of James Franciscus's television series, "Longstreet." Much has been written about this fabulous house and its almost magical spiral staircase. But Houmas House is actually two houses: the four-room cottage to the rear was built in the late 18th century on land purchased from the Houmas Indians, and the main house went up in 1840.

Make it a point to stop in **The Cabin** for lunch on your plantation prowl. The word "picturesque" could properly have been coined for this unique restaurant, a cluster of 150-year-old slave dwellings with massive cypress beams and walls papered with ancient newspapers. The (modern) restrooms are enclosed in huge cypress water cisterns. The menu is a happy blend of po-boys and porkchops, crawfish and steak, at prices from $4 to $12, and is very highly recommended. It's at the juncture of highways 22 and 44—you'll know when you get there by a big sign which says, "You're Here!"

Three West Bank plantations offer overnight accommodations. Two are on the River Road, and one is on Bayou LaFourche (pronounced *la foósh*).

Nottoway (on La. 1; 504–545–2730) will knock your socks off. The nearby little town of White Castle was named for this 64-room white castle, the 1859 creation of architect Henry Howard. If you've seen one plantation, you've not by any means seen them all. Each is different, and Nottoway is in a class by itself. The great white masterpiece has about 53,000 square feet of space, 22 huge white columns, and a white ballroom which is a legend hereabouts. Ten of its

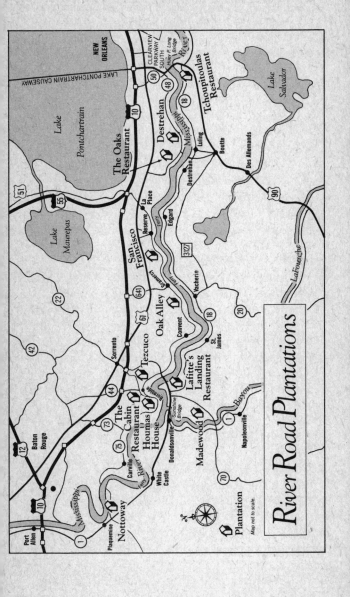

River Road Plantations

rooms are let to overnight guests. The double rate of
$115 to $135 includes many frills, among them a
chilled bottle of champagne awaiting you in your
room. Nottoway's restaurant is open daily for lunch
from 11 A.M. to 3 P.M. and for dinner from 6:30 to 8
P.M. at fixed prices of $9 and $15, respectively.

To the south of Nottoway is another Henry Howard triumph. The 21-room Greek Revival **Madewood**
(Hwy. 308, in Napoleonville; 504–524–1988) graces
the banks of Bayou LaFourche, and was about 138
years old when it appeared in *A Woman Called Moses,* a
movie starring Cicely Tyson. Overnight guests in the
main house ($150 per couple) are entertained in the
grand manner. A separate plantation on the premises
and a small slave quarters each have two-bedroom
suites which can be had for $85 per couple. **Oak Alley**
is also a movie star, having been the setting for the
1985 television adaptation of *The Long Hot Summer.*
The plantation was christened *Bon Sejour* by its builder
in 1837, but riverboat passengers who saw it always
remarked about the splendid alley of oaks, so the
name was eventually changed. In the early 1700s, an
unknown French settler built a small cottage where
the present mansion is, and planted 28 oaks—14 on
each side of the approach to the house from River
Road. Overnight guests stay in three two-bedroom
cabins on the grounds ($60 to $75 per couple), and a
restaurant in one of the cabins is open daily for lunch
from 11 A.M. to 3 P.M. ($6 to $9). You'll need a reservation for Oak Alley's annual Christmas Bonfire Party,
which features jazz, gumbo, and a big bonfire on the
levee.

In this part of South Louisiana, the tradition of
Christmas bonfires on the levees dates back to when
the area was first settled. Residents on both sides of
the river gather wood, cane, and trash to make enormous stacks, some of them two stories high. On

Christmas Eve, the huge piles are torched and the flaming bonfires light the way for Papa Noel. Don't miss it if you're in the neighborhood at Christmastime.

If you've a couple of days to spare, you'll have a wonderful time exploring Cajun Country. Also called Acadiana, Cajun Country is comprised of 22 parishes in southwestern Louisiana. Just as New Orleans is unique, there's no place in the country like Acadiana. The area was settled by French-speaking Acadians who migrated here in the mid-18th century after being expelled by the British from their homeland in what is now the Canadian province of Nova Scotia. That arduous exodus was poignantly described in Longfellow's poem *Evangeline*. Proudly calling themselves Cajuns, their descendants speak an antique 17th-century form of French and their carefree spirit is summed up in the Acadiana motto, *"Laissez les bon temps rouler!"* (let the good times roll). There is always big, big fun on the bayou.

The capital of Acadiana is **Lafayette,** 150 miles west of New Orleans. The fastest route is via I-10 West. Once there, head for the **Visitor Information Center** on Evangeline Thruway at 16th Street. Load up the tote bag with maps and brochures, chat with the friendly Cajun staff, and set out for an unforgettable adventure. Just as the bayous wind lazily through the countryside, you should meander along the state and parish roads. You'll pass folks poling pirogues down the bayous, cabins perched on stilts high above the marshes, "floating prairies" of canebrakes, and spectacular scenery reminiscent of the Amazon.

Lafayette offers a number of interesting attractions. A great introduction to Cajun Country is the **Acadian Village** (Mouton Road; 318–981–2364), a recreation of an early bayou settlement. Several rustic cypress cabins were built elsewhere in the early 19th century and transferred to the ten idyllic acres. Wooden footbridges criss-cross a lazy bayou, which mirrors moss-trimmed trees, and Cajun fiddles often tune up and take off on the side porch of the General Store. All of the facilities of the 117-acre **Nature Park** are free. Naturalists are on hand in the three-story Nature Station, and the 40-acre Nature Trail is particularly spectacular in this neck of the bayou. There's pari-mutuel betting and racing with a Cajun flair at **Evangeline Downs,** where each race begins with *"Ils sont partis!"* In late March or early April, the **Azalea Trail** is ablaze with blossoms (one of the attractions along the way is **Bendel Gardens,** on the site of the birthplace of department store tycoon Henri Bendel), and September is the month of the freewheeling **Festivals Acadiens.** *Les bon temps* roll like crazy during Lafayette's four-day Mardi Gras celebration. **Cajun Carnival** is ruled by King Gabriel and Queen Evangeline, and on Fat Tuesday anybody and everybody second-lines behind the parade of the Krewe of Lafayette in a grand and glorious street festival.

Be sure to take your camera when you drive over to **McGee's Landing** in nearby Henderson, where you can hook up with a tour that explores some of the 800,000 acres of the **Atchalafaya Basin.** The rich wilderness is a scenic wonderland of hardwood forests and cypress swamps, migratory birds, deer, cougar, and alligator, and the fishing is great.

Find out where there's a *fais-do-do,* drop whatever you're doing, and *go!* That's a Cajun dance, and it's as much a part of Cajun life as crawfish pie. Pick up a copy of *The Times of Acadiana,* turn to the calendar, and run your finger down the *Musique* listing. You'll probably see *Bal fais-do-do* doings at Kootzie's Lounge, to the west of Lafayette in Rayne, and at *La Poussiere* in Breaux Bridge to the east. The *fais-do-do* is a family affair, but you'll be "family" as soon as you set foot in the door.

Make a beeline for **Mulate's** in Breaux Bridge, 15 minutes outside of Lafayette on Highway 94. It's a Cajun café, a beer joint, a dance hall, and a family gathering place. It's been featured on five television documentaries in the past two years, not to mention the "Today Show" and "Good Morning, America." (This translates into big crowds. You might avoid them on a Sunday night when the crowd is mostly hard-core regulars.) Cajun is all the rage these days, but Mulate's has been going strong for almost 75 years.

St. Martinville was once known as "Petite Paris" because of the aristocrats who sought refuge there during the French Revolution, but it's best known for the legend of *Evangeline*. Longfellow's poem was based on real-life lovers, Emmeline Labiche and Louis Arceneaux. At Port Street and Bayou Teche you'll find the Evangeline Oak and, poised on the bayou's bank, a graceful gazebo. According to the legend, this was the last meeting place of the star-crossed lovers. North of town on Highway 31, the **Longfellow-Evangeline Commemorative Area** is believed by some to be on land that once belonged to Louis Arceneaux. You can poke through the **Acadian House Museum,** built circa 1765, and picnic on the glorious grounds. **St. Martin de Tours,** Mother Church of the Acadians, is on Main Street, and behind it is a statue of Evangeline for which Dolores del Rio posed. *The Romance of Evangeline* was filmed in St. Martinville in 1929, with Ms. Del Rio as the star, and the cast and crew donated the statue to the town. You won't starve for Cajun music in St. Martinville. There's a live stage show every Saturday night at the **St. Martinville Opry House,** and you should hang around for the dance following it.

New Iberia is a pretty little town founded in the mid 18th century by Spaniards who named it for their homeland on the Iberian coast. It boasts two lovely plantations—**Shadows on the Teche** (318–369–6446) and **Mintmere** (318–364–6210)—both of which are on Main Street and open to the public. Just off Main Street you can board the *Teche Queen* for a paddlewheel cruise down the long-ago main drag of the Attakapas and Chitimacha Indians. One of the largest bayous in Louisiana, Bayou Teche snakes through forests in some places so thick the sun's rays can barely squeeze through the leaves. Other sights in the Queen City of the Teche are the **Gebert Oak,** and a seven-foot white marble statue of the **Emperor Hadrian,** sculpted in Rome in A.D. 130. You can tour **Konriko,** the country's oldest rice mill, and on nearby **Avery Island** visit the Tabasco factory, birthplace of the hot sauce that flavors many a Bloody Mary. Avery Island is a 300-acre paradise with a Jungle Garden, a 1,000-year-old Buddha seated serenely in a pagoda, exotic plants in blossom virtually the year round, and a bird sanctuary sometimes almost solid white with egrets. At Louisiana highways 14 and 675, the 20-acre **Live Oak Gardens** surround the winter home built in 1870 by American actor Joseph Jefferson. On its grounds are picnic areas, a Japanese Tea Garden, Alhambra Garden, Camellia Garden, and a two-mile lane of live oaks. Jefferson wrote, "In Louisiana the live oak is king of the forest, the magnolia is queen, and there is nothing finer to one fond of the country than to sit under them on calm clear spring mornings."

The last thing you need worry about in Acadiana is food. As noted, Cajun cooking is the robust country cousin of Creole cuisine, and in this part of the world food and fun are synonymous. You'll find good food every time you turn around. Your ultimate concern is a place to stay. Lafayette is loaded with familiar chain inns, and Beno's Motel in St. Martinville is a big modern place with king-sized and double beds, cable TV, a pool, restaurant, and double rooms for $35 per night. **Louisiana Hospitality Services** can book you into a country inn and will do so without charging you a fee (contact them at Box 80717, Baton Rouge, Louisiana 70898).

Index